Praise for *Truth* ~~about Adventist~~ *Truth*

Seventh-day Adventist teachings are rapidly spreading around the world. For decades there has been a need for a clear and concise biblical examination of the fundamental teachings of this church. This ready reference on Adventism compares biblical Christianity with contemporary Adventism and quickly gives the reader an understanding of the major issues and answers. *Truth about Adventist "Truth"* is a ministry tool that will equip many to meet the questions of those interested in Adventism as well as share the Gospel with the searching thousands within the Seventh-day Adventist Church.—**J. Mark Martin, Senior Pastor, Calvary Community Church, Phoenix, Arizona.**

Every true Christ-follower wants to be among those who are described as "more noble" because they "examine the Scriptures daily to see if these things were so." Dale Ratzlaff's helpful little booklet will force many to look carefully to see whether what they have been taught is really what God's Word says. I am so thankful that God has used Dale's ministry to bring many into the glorious freedom of the gospel that God desires for his people. —**Gary Inrig, Senior Pastor, Trinity Evangelical Free Church, Redlands, California**

I was among the many Christians to whom Dale refers, who believed that the Seventh Day Adventist Church was simply another evangelical denomination. As a pastor, I have found myself ill-equipped to respond. Through this very helpful and well-documented handbook, I learned that Adventists bear many of the distinguishing marks of a cult; founded on heretical views of the Trinity, strict legalism, a leader who is considered an "authoritative *source* of truth," adding to Scripture and the claim that they are "the remnant." I have also learned how to respond with grace and truth. I have come to know Dale and Carolyn as people who deeply care about graciously helping Adventists transition from an oppressive, legalistic religious system to enjoying the freedom of the simple Gospel of Christ.—**John Amandola, Jr., Senior Pastor, Lake Pleasant Community Church, Peoria, Arizona**

There are certain hurdles, roadblocks or blinders (call them what you will) that keep an Adventist from seeing the truth of the gospel of the free grace of Jesus Christ. These roadblocks must first be dealt with before an Adventist can move from legalism to liberty. This "Truth" booklet does that very thing. It is short, concise and to the point—a handbook of sorts with a dual purpose. First, to reach Adventists with information that is tailor made just for them; and second, to equip the Christian man or woman to be effective when reaching out to his/her Adventist friend. I highly recommend this book and commend Dale Ratzlaff for this informative work.—**David H. Soto, Pastor, Cabazon Fellowship Church, Cabazon, California**

About the Author

Dale Ratzlaff was a conservative, fourth generation Seventh-day Adventist (SDA). He received all his formal education in SDA schools, graduated from the Seventh-day Adventist seminary, pastored two Seventh-day Adventist churches, and taught Bible in a Seventh-day Adventist school for seven years. In the 1980s, while nearing the end of his doctoral program at Andrews University, he became convinced that the SDA doctrine of the investigative judgment and cleansing of the heavenly sanctuary could not be supported by Scripture, was contrary to clear biblical teaching and undermined the new covenant gospel of grace. His conference president told him that he either had to promise to teach all of the Fundamental Beliefs of the SDA church or resign. Because he could not do this in clear conscience, Pastor Ratzlaff with his wife Carolyn, who was a denominationally employed Bible worker, left the SDA denomination. Since that time, Pastor Ratzlaff has written four books dealing with Adventist issues.

In 2000 Dale and Carolyn Ratzlaff, working with Richard and Colleen Tinker, started Life Assurance Ministries, Inc., a non-profit corporation that publishes the bi-monthly journal, *Proclamation!* which is sent free of charge to approximately 35,000 homes at this writing. This has been a faith ministry from its inception.

Dale Ratzlaff also manages LAM Publications, LLC which publishes and sells a number of books written by former Adventists. These combined ministries have helped thousands make the difficult transition from Adventism to healthy evangelical churches.

Truth about Adventist "Truth"

Dale Ratzlaff

Truth about Adventist "Truth"

Second printing, 2000
Third printing, 2001
Fourth printing and revision, 2005
Fifth printing, second revision, new ISBN, 2007

LAM Publications, LLC
PO Box 11587, Glendale, Arizona 85318
800-355-7073, Email: dale@ratzlaf.com
Web Site: www.LifeAssuranceMinistries.com

Library of Congress Control Number: 2007909242

ISBN 0-9747679-4-8

Printed in the United States of America

Dedication

To all the former Adventists who were brave enough to search out the foundations of their faith; who believe that truth needs no other foundation than honest investigation under the guidance of the Holy Spirit, and a willingness to follow truth when it is revealed; who found the simple new covenant gospel of God's grace and measured their life and theology by its truth.

Contents

Foreword

One cannot help but be impressed by the progress of Seventh-day Adventism in our day. Its colleges and universities produce legions of graduates, its medical institutions are centers of innovation and healing. The legacy of Ellen G. White lives on through her "health message," through the denomination's global missionary endeavors, and through parachurch agencies such as *Amazing Facts, The Voice of Prophecy*, and *The Quiet Hour*.

Yet many Christians are, at best, vaguely aware that Adventism is somehow—different. And so this booklet challenges the reader to ask and answer two central questions for himself: Are the differences real? And if so, do they matter?

The time for a reassessment among evangelicals is long overdue, because for too many inattentive Christians, Adventism represents a profound danger hidden in plain sight. As Dale Ratzlaff amply demonstrates in the following pages, the movement is founded not on the infallible Word of God, but on such an extraordinary mass of error and calculated deception that it must be seen to be believed. The differences between Adventism and biblical Christianity cannot be ignored, for they strike at the very heart of the gospel. The disciples of Ellen G. White do not merely offer an alternative view of secondary Christian doctrines, as many suppose; instead, they encourage millions to place their trust in a false prophet who sets obstacles in the path of anyone who would trust in Christ alone for their salvation and "adds" nothing to the written Word of God except her convoluted and contradictory speculations.

The evidence presented herein compels evangelicals to make an informed choice. Pastors, missionaries, relief agencies, and others need to face the potential problems of collaborating, on an organizational level, with a movement that affirms and promotes such error. Many of us who have served as missionaries in the Third World recognize the two faces of Adventism: indulging in cozy ecumenism in English-speaking cultures while engaging in bare-knuckle proselytizing nearly everywhere else. The Seventh-day Adventist Church cannot have it both ways.

As those who have been commanded to "test all things" (1 Thess. 5:21) and "defend the faith once for all delivered to the saints" (Jude 3–4), we have neither the liberty nor the luxury of turning a blind eye to these matters. To do so means not only unconscionable compromise for evangelicals, but spiritual bondage for countless Adventists who need to hear the Gospel proclaimed as God intended.

In closing, let me assure the reader that this booklet is no mere rant or rebuke. It is a message motivated by compassion, given in the sincere hope that through a careful presentation of the evidence many who are held captive by Adventism will one day be "free indeed" (Jn. 8:36).

Paul Carden, Executive Director
The Centers for Apologetics Research
San Juan Capistrano, California

Preface

We as former Adventists are often asked why we write material which appears to be attacking the Seventh-day Adventist Church. Many current Adventist leaders from all levels of the SDA denomination have been in communication with our ministry and have encouraged us to keep doing what we are doing. Most of these people are aware that there are many embedded errors in Adventism; nevertheless they remain in the SDA church for one or more of the following reasons: (1) to help Adventists understand the gospel; (2) to change the church from the inside; (3) to stay for job security and retirement; or (4) to stay for family and reputation. These people wish to remain anonymous and we will grant their request.

Thousands of former Seventh-day Adventists who have made the transition to the simple gospel of Christ and have become Bible-only believers have expressed to us the joy of the freedom they experience in Christ. They have a deep desire to help free others from the bondage of Adventism.

In seeking to promote change we want to be kind to our "mother church", yet we must be open and honest in facing the errors that are embedded in Adventism. From our perspective it appears that the Adventist church is like a chameleon. In its public relations it seeks to appear as a mainstream Christian church. Yet in the latter stages of most Adventist evangelism or doctrinal teaching, it claims that the Seventh-day Adventist church is the "remnant church of Bible prophecy" and that the seventh-day Sabbath is the seal of God which all true believers must have in order to escape the seven last plagues. It teaches that the Catholic Church is the harlot in the book of Revelation and that Protestant churches which worship on Sunday are the "daughters of Babylon", and in the last days all true Christians are to be called out of churches which worship on Sunday so they will not receive the mark of the beast.

Today there is a virtual mandate that evangelicals not only understand the errors of Adventism, but learn how to minister to the approximately 300,000 Adventists who leave the SDA church every year.[1] It is our prayer that this little book will be a useful first step in this regard.

This book is not intended to be an in-depth evaluation of the errors of Adventism. Rather, its purpose is to give a sweeping overview of these errors with enough documentation to support the statements made therein. As I have written several other books and dozens of articles on these topics, I have often noted where the reader may find a more exhaustive study of the topic at hand. I have at times listed an internet website as the source for a given statement. I recognize that these may be somewhat dynamic and subject to change. If you can't find a given site, try searching on Google.

For those who wish to develop a much needed ministry to transitioning Adventists, or desire to study Adventism more deeply, I suggest that you consult the many resources listed in the back of this book including the many internet websites. Be sure and read "The Transitional Path" on my web site at: www.LifeAssuranceMinistries.com/trpath.html

In His joy,

Dale Ratzlaff

---

[1] See http://news.adventist.org/data/2005/06/1120249432/index.html.en

Chapter
ONE

Ellen White, a Source of Truth

Ellen White as a *source* of truth is perhaps *the* underlying error of the SDA church. Fundamental Belief No. 18 includes the following statement.

> ...As the Lord's messenger, her [Ellen G. White's] writings are a continuing and authoritative *source* of truth which provide for the church comfort, guidance, instruction, and correction. They also make clear that the Bible is the standard by which all teaching and experience must be tested.[1] (emphasis added)

Officially, Adventists believe the writings of Ellen G. White (EGW) are inspired on the same level as the Bible.[2] Because she is the later inspired writer, many SDAs hold that her interpretation of the Bible is to be preferred over the meaning the biblical text itself conveys.[3] While it is true

---

[1] For a list of the 28 Fundamental Beliefs of the Seventh-day Adventists, see: www.adventist.org/beliefs/fundamental/index.html

[2] In recent years much new evidence has surfaced which demonstrates the many problems associated with the writings of Ellen White. In order to keep these as "inspired writings," SDAs have had to liberalize their concept of inspiration to allow for such things as massive plagiarism, historical errors, suppressed visions, inaccurate statements, and contradictions to the Bible.

[3] "Adventists who deny this historic equation (Bible study + EGW confirmation = Adventist distinctives), for whatever reason, are forced to go back into the confusion....To ignore history would put us back to the same uncertain playing field where all other churches are each contending that it alone believes in 'the Bible and the Bible alone.' The deep doctrinal struggles within Evangelicalism today are fought by

that the writings of EGW contain some good material,[4] it is equally true that they contain gross error.[5] Her early writings[6] are legalistic and very condemning of nearly all other churches. She saw the Catholic Church as "Babylon" and the "Harlot" of Revelation and the Protestant churches which did not accept SDAs unique teaching on the three angels' messages of Revelation 14 as "fallen churches" and the "daughters of Babylon."[7]

Ellen White did not invent SDA erroneous theology, but she cemented it into the foundation of Adventism. The writings of Ellen White support, and are often the chief support, for all of their unbiblical doctrines. And here is the Adventist dilemma: many within Adventism would like to jettison EGW as "a continuing and authoritative source of truth" and the unbiblical doctrines supported by her writings. To do so, however, would cause a serious crisis in Adventism. To avoid this crisis, Adventist leadership has used over a dozen different tactics of dealing with known error without ever admitting to the error.[8]

---

strongly convinced men and women who believe their positions rest on the Bible only. Without Ellen White, that same impasse would continue to fragment the Adventist denomination." Quoted from Robert S. Folkenburg, *From the G.C. President,* "Off the Back Burner," January, 22–April 22, 1996.

[4] Much of the best material is copied from others. See Walter T. Rea, *White Lie,* (M & R Publicaitons, Box 2056, Turlock, CA 95381).

[5] See Ratzlaff, *Cultic Doctrine;* Anderson, *White Out* and Cleveland, *White Washed* for many examples. (All published by LAM Publications, LLC, PO Box 11587, Glendale, AZ 85318).

[6] *Early Writings* is a title of one of EGW's books. However, I use the term here to include all of her early writings, many of which contain serious, even heretical, error.

[7] Ellen G. White, *Spiritual Gifts,* Vol. 1, pp. 135, 140, 155, 156, 169, 172.

[8] *Cultic Doctrine,* see chapter, "Lumps Under the Rug".

It is incredible that SDAs still hold the writings of Ellen G. White to be authoritative and inspired on the same level as Jeremiah and other Old Testament prophets.[9] Consider the following questionable, unbiblical, or even heretical statements.

> We are placed here on probation to see if we will prove worthy of eternal life.[10]

> For a period of time Christ was on probation. He took humanity on himself, to stand the test and trial which the first Adam failed to endure. Had he failed in His test and trial, He would have been disobedient to the voice of God, and the world would have been lost.[11]

> Those who accept the Saviour, however sincere their conversion, should never be taught to say or to feel that they are saved.[12]

> A view of things was presented before me in which the students were playing games of tennis and cricket. Then I was given instruction regarding the character of these amusements. They were presented to me as a species of idolatry, like the idols of the nations.[13]

> Since the flood there has been amalgamation [sexual union] of man and beast, as may be seen in the almost endless varieties of species of animals, and in certain races of men.[14]

Jesus had *older* brothers. [15] (emphasis added)

Ellen White gave a number of failed prophecies[16] including the statement that "Old Jerusalem would never be built up."[17]

---

[9] *Review & Harold,* 1928-5-11.

[10] Ellen G. White, *Testimonies for the Church,* Vol. 1, p. 198.

[11] Ellen G. White, *SDA Bible Commentary,* p. 1082.

[12] Ellen G. White, *Christ Object Lessons,* p. 155.

[13] Ellen G. White, *Counsels to Teachers,* p. 350.

[14] *Spiritual Gifts,* Vol. 3, p. 75.

[15] Ellen G. White, *The Desire of Ages,* p. 87.

Regarding the wearing of wigs, she said, "Many have lost their reason, and become hopelessly insane, by following this deforming fashion."[18]

Ellen white wrote that Satan had taken full possession of the churches which rejected Adventist's reinterpretation of the failed 1844 prophecy.[19]

Ellen White said,

In these letters which I write, in the testimonies I bear, I am presenting to you that which the Lord has presented to me. I do not write one article in the paper expressing merely my own ideas. They are what God has opened before me in vision—the precious rays of light shining from the throne.[20]

I have the most precious matter to reproduce and place before the people in testimony form. While I am able to do this work, the people must have these things, to revive past truth, *without one heretical sentence, in that which I have written*. This, I am instructed, is to be a living letter to all in regard to my faith.[21] (emphasis added)

Our Faith Founded on Truth...I have been pleading with the Lord for strength and wisdom to reproduce the writings of the witnesses who were *confirmed in the faith* and in the early history of the message. After the passing of the time in *1844, they received the light* and walked in the light, and when the men claiming to have new light would come in with their wonderful messages regarding *various points of Scripture,* we had, through the moving of the Holy Spirit, *testimonies right to the point,* which **cut off the influence** of such messages.

When the power of God testifies as to what is truth, that truth is to stand forever as the truth. No after-suppositions, contrary to the light God has given are to be entertained. Men

---

[16] See *White Washed* and *White Out,* for a number of other illustrations of White's failed prophecies.

[17] *Early Writings,* p. 75.

[18] Ellen G. White, *Review & Harold,* 1871-10.

[19] *Spiritual Gifts,* Vol. 1, p. 189.

[20] *Testimonies for the Church,* Vol. 5, p. 67.

[21] Paulson Collection of Ellen G. White's letters, 019.007.

will arise with *interpretations of Scripture* which are to them truth, but which are not truth. ***The truth for this time, God has given us as a foundation for our faith. He Himself has taught us what is truth.*** One will arise, and still another with new light, which contradicts the light that God has given under the demonstration of His Holy Spirit. A few are still alive who passed through the experience gained in the establishment of this truth. God has graciously spared their lives to repeat and repeat till the close of their lives, the *experience through which they passed* even as did John the apostle till the very close of his life. And the *standard bearers* who have fallen in death, are to speak through the reprinting of their writings. *I am instructed* that thus their voices are to be heard. *They are to bear their testimony as to what constitutes the truth for this time.*

We are not to receive the words of those who come with a message that contradicts the special points of our faith. They gather together *a mass of Scripture,* and pile it as proof around their asserted theories. This has been done over and over again during the past fifty years. *And while the Scriptures are God's Word, and are to be respected, the application of them,* ***if such application moves one pillar from the foundation that God has sustained these fifty years, is a great mistake.*** He who makes such an application knows not the wonderful demonstration of the Holy Spirit that gave power and force to the past messages that have come to the people of God.[22] (emphasis added)

The above quote penned in 1904 demonstrates the cultic heart of Adventism. Adventist "truth" is *primarily* founded on the early *experience* of those who went through the 1844 debacle. Further, Ellen White makes it patently clear that this so-called "truth" that was *confirmed* "through the moving of the Holy Spirit" (her visions and testimonies) is the plumb line to which any interpretation of Scripture must be aligned. This is clearly placing her writings

---

[22] Ellen G. White, *Notebook Leaflets from the Elmshaven Library,* 1904, p. 157. See also *Paulson Collection of Ellen White Letters,* p. 208.

as a *"source* of truth" over the witness of Scripture, something no Christian, at least no Protestant Christian, would ever do!

Today, Adventist leadership realizes that the church needs the writings of Ellen White more than ever. About 300,000 Adventists are leaving the SDA church *every year.*[23] In what appears to be a desperate attempt to stop the exodus, the denomination has launched "Connecting With Jesus".

> The largest global book distribution project in the history of the Seventh-day Adventist Church…Sponsored by the General Conference and the world divisions in cooperation with the Ellen G. White Estate, the project entitled "Connecting With Jesus" will provide ten Ellen White books with study guides to two million Adventist families around the world during a five year period. The books and study guides will be published in many languages at subsidized prices that all can afford….In the beginning of the Advent movement, God worked through Ellen White to help shape the mission and message of the church. Making these heaven-sent messages available to new church members, as well as to others who do not now have access to them, will help assure the on-going unity of the church, both theologically and organizationally.[24]

While the Adventist church claims to be a Bible based church, the leaders know very well that Bible study without Ellen White interpretation will lead members out of the church. Her writings serve as a prism through which Adventists interpret Scripture. This is why it is imperative for questioning Adventists to determine once and for all the veracity of the writings of Ellen White. Unless they lay aside her writings, they will be unable to see the unity and truth of Scripture.[25]

---

[23] http://news.adventist.org/data/2005/06/1120249432/index.html.en
[24] http://www.connectingwithjesus.org
[25] This has been confirmed by the author in conversations with hundreds of former Seventh-day Adventists.

Chapter
TWO

Founded on Error and Deception

The founders of Adventism were followers of William Miller who, by the dubious method of proof-texting, predicted that Christ was going to return in 1843. When He did not, the Millerites revised the date to October 22, 1844. Miller had some 15 "proofs" to back up his dates and a large chart which pictured the beasts of Daniel and Revelation along with his calculations. Of Miller's chart, Ellen White wrote:

> I have seen that the 1843 chart was directed by the hand of the Lord, and that it should not be altered; that the figures were as He wanted them.[1]

She also made some very bold statements about Christian pastors who did not accept Miller's date-setting message.

> I saw that God was in the proclamation of the time in 1843. It was His design to arouse the people and bring them to a testing point, where they should decide for or against *the truth*. Thousands were led to embrace *the truth* preached by William Miller.[2] (emphasis added)

> Many shepherds of the flock, who professed to love Jesus, said that they had *no opposition to the preaching of Christ's coming, but they objected to the definite time.*[3] (emphasis added)

---

[1] *Early Writings,* p. 74.
[2] Ibid., p. 232.
[3] Ibid., p. 234.

> Ministers who would not accept this *saving message* [note that in context, this "saving message" refers to the acceptance of a "definite time"] themselves hindered those who would have received it. *The blood of souls is upon them.* Preachers and people joined to oppose this *message from heaven* and to persecute William Miller and those who united with him in the work. [4] (emphasis added)

October 22, 1844, is a pivotal date in Adventism. It is known as "the great disappointment" because Christ did not return as predicted. However, rather than admit error, Adventists re-interpreted the failed prophecy of Miller[5] and taught that instead of coming to earth on that date as they had predicted, Christ entered for the *first time* into the Most Holy Place of the heavenly sanctuary.[6] They understood this to mean that the door to the first apartment, where Adventists said forgiveness was offered, was now shut. Thus Adventists taught that the "door of mercy" was shut for all the churches which rejected this new "truth" and for the whole "wicked world whom God had rejected".

> I saw that the nominal churches [those who had rejected the 1844 sanctuary message], as the Jews crucified Jesus, had crucified these messages, and therefore they have no knowledge of the move made in heaven, or of the way into the Most Holy, and *they cannot be benefited by the intercession of Jesus* there. Like the Jews, who offered their useless sacrifices, they offer up their *useless prayers* to the apartment which Jesus has left, and Satan, pleased with the deception of the professed followers of Christ, fastens them in his snare, and assumes a religious character, and leads the minds of these professed

---

[4] Ibid., p. 234.
[5] Miller did admit to the error and did not support the "shut door" Adventists who re-interpreted his prophecy.
[6] Chapter 6 will have more information on these events. See Ratzlaff, *Cultic Doctrine* for a full description of these events.

Christians to himself, and works with his power, his signs and lying wonders. [7] (emphasis added)

As the years went by, however, in order to get their own children who were born after 1844 into the "shut door" of salvation, they had to re-interpret their re-interpretation of their revised prophecy of the failed prophecy. In order to pry open the "shut door of mercy" they revised their definition of "door" [8] and the timing of when it was shut without ever renouncing their early errors. [9]

To keep the early errors upon which Adventism was founded "out of sight" they used several types of deception. For example, they have suppressed one of Ellen White's visions because it clearly teaches a shut door of salvation after 1844. [10] Her first vision is printed in the book, *Early Writings.* What many Adventists do not know is that part of this vision has been deleted even though the preface says,

> No change has been made in any idea or sentiment of the original work, and the verbal changes have been made under the author's own eye, and with her full approval. [11]

There were some Adventists [12] who still had her original vision as published in *A Word to the Little Flock* which included the "shut door" statements. These people accused

---

[7] *Early Writings,* p. 261.

[8] The "door" went from Mt. 25:10 to Rev. 3:8. See *Cultic Doctrine,* the chapter, "The Swinging Door".

[9] For a more in-depth discussion and documentation of these events see, *Cultic Doctrine,* the chapters, "Truth Changes Again" and "The Swinging Door".

[10] *Cultic Doctrine,* p. 129, 130; D. M Canright, *The Life of Mrs. E.G. White,* p. 149, 150 (original paging) p. 86, 87 (reprint paging; Published by Grant Shurtliff, Sterling Press, Salt Lake City, UT, 1998).

[11] Preface to *Early Writings,* p. 3.

[12] Elder A. C. Long, See *The Life of Mrs. E.G. White,* p. 147 (original paging), p. 85 (reprint paging).

the church leaders of suppression. Adventist leader Elder G.I. Butler said such charges were "lying insinuations".[13]

Here is a portion of Ellen White's first vision as printed in *A Word to the Little Flock.* I have bolded the words which were left out of this vision as published in *Early Writings.*

> Others rashly denied the light behind them, [their Millerite experience] and said that it was not God that had led them out so far. The light behind them went out leaving their feet in perfect darkness, and they stumbled and got their eyes off the mark and lost sight of Jesus, and fell off the path down in the dark and wicked world below. ***It was just as impossible for them to get on the path again and go to the City, as all the wicked world which God had rejected. They fell all the way along the path one after another, until*** we heard the voice of God like many waters, which gave us the day and hour of Jesus' coming.

When honest Adventist leaders learned of some of these errors and left the church, they were usually castigated and given over to Satan.[14]

W.W. Prescott, an early, respected leader in Adventism, in his later years wrote:

> It seems to me that we are betraying our trust and *deceiving the ministers and the people.* It appears to me that there is much more anxiety to prevent a possible shock than to correct error.[15] (emphasis added)

Prescott also wrote the following in a letter addressed to Ellen White's son, Willie White.

> It seems to me that a large responsibly rests upon those of us who know that there are *serious errors in our authorized books* [books written by Ellen G. White] and yet make no

---

[13] Ibid.

[14] Ibid., See also *Cultic Doctrine*, p. 186f.

[15] Gilbert M. Valentine, *The Shaping of Adventism,* (Berrien Springs, MI, Andrews University Press, 1992) p. 215–229.

special effort to correct them. The people and our average ministers trust us to furnish them with reliable statements, and they use our books as sufficient authority in their sermons, but we let them go on year after year asserting things which we know to be untrue. I cannot feel this is right...the way your mother's writings have been handled and the false impression concerning them which is still fostered among the people have brought great perplexity and trial to me. *It seems to me that what amounts to deception...has been practiced in making some of her books and no serious effort has been made to disabuse the minds of the people of what was known to be their wrong view concerning her writings.* But it is no use to go into these matters, I have talked with you for years about them, but it brings no change. [16] (emphasis added)

Elder J. N. Loughborough, in his book, *The Great Second Adventist Movement,* endeavoring to support the ministry of Ellen White, quoted Elder Joseph Bates' early endorsement of her writings.

I believe the work [of Mrs. White] is of God, and is given to comfort and strengthen his scattered, torn and peeled people, since the closing up of our work...in October 1844. [17]

Do you wonder what Loughborough left out of Bates' testimony? Just three little words but these three words confirmed the belief in the shut door of salvation that Loughborough was trying to suppress:

...since the closing up of our work **for the world** in October 1844. [18]

---

[16] Ibid, See also, Ford, *Daniel 8:14, The Day of Atonement and The Investigative Judgment,* (Euangelioin Press, P.O. box 1264, Casselberry, FL), p. 370.

[17] See *The Life of Mrs. E. G. White,* p. 163-165 (original) p. 94 (re-printed).

[18] Ibid.

The way early Adventist leaders dealt with known error seems to be the template the church has used and continues to use to this day:

- Suppress the early errors.
- Do not respond to those who point out the errors.
- Never admit to the errors.
- Cast out all who expose the errors.
- Tell Adventist members they will be deceived by Satan if they read the writings of those who point out the errors of Adventism.[19]
- Tell Adventist members they will lose their salvation if they reject the writings of Ellen White and leave Adventism.

> It is Satan's plan to weaken the faith of God's people in the *Testimonies* [writings of Ellen White]. Next follows skepticism in regard to the vital points of our faith, the pillars of our position, then doubt as to the Holy Scriptures, and then the downward march to perdition. When the *Testimonies*, which were once believed are doubted and given up, Satan knows the deceived ones will not stop at this; and he redoubles his efforts till he launches them into open rebellion, which becomes incurable and ends in destruction.[20]

Not only did the founding Adventists organize themselves around the heresies of date-setting and false doctrines designed to cover their mistakes, but they denied the Trinity and rejected the full deity of Christ. They taught that Jesus was Michael the archangel[21] Note the following quotes from Ellen White.

---

[19] See *Daniel 8:14,* p. 44 for a number of illustrations.

[20] *Testimonies for the Church,* Vol. 4, p. 211.

[21] Christ resurrected Moses, and took him to Heaven. This enraged Satan, and he accused the Son of God of invading his dominion by robbing the grave of his lawful prey. Jude says of the resurrection of Moses, "Yet Michael the archangel, when contending with the devil, he disputed about the body of Moses, durst not bring against him a railing

> The ministry of the angel at the altar of incense [in Rev. 3:8] is representative of Christ's intercession.[22]

> The mighty angel who instructed John [in Rev. 1:1] was no less than the person of Christ.[23]

> The man Christ Jesus was not the Lord God Almighty.[24]

> To Christ had been given an exalted position. He has been made equal with the Father.[25]

The above quotes reveal the Arian teachings that Jesus was not eternally divine, but was later promoted to a high position with God.

> In swearing by the creator, the angel [in Rev. 10:5, 6] who is Christ, swore by himself.[26]

When we contrast this teaching to the words of Christ we see how serious it is to undermine the full deity of Christ.

> Therefore I said to you that you will die in your sins; for unless you believe that I am *He*, you will die in your sins.[27]

> Jesus said to them, "Truly, truly, I say to you, before Abraham was born, I am."[28]

In the above texts Jesus says that unless we believe what He says about Himself, we will die in our sins. Then He says, "Before Abraham, "I am", indicating that He is the

---

accusation, but said, The Lord rebuke thee." Ellen G. White, *Redemption,* Vol. 2, p 24, See also, *Testimonies for the Church,* Vol. 3, p. 220; *Review & Herald,* 1874-03-03; 1886-03-23.

[22] Ellen G. White, *Manuscript 15,* 1897.

[23] Ellen G. White, *Manuscript 59,* 1900.

[24] Ellen G. White, *Manuscript 150; SDA Bible Commentary,* Vol. 5, p. 1129, 1903.

[25] Ellen G. White, *Testimonies for the Church,* Vol. 8, p. 268, 1904.

[26] Ellen G. White, *SDA Bible Commentary,* Vol. 7, p, 798, 1905.

[27] John 8:24.

[28] John 5:58.

eternally, self-existent One. It is no small thing to degrade the deity of Christ.

Early Adventists also saw the Trinity as an erroneous doctrine.[29] Adventist leader R.F. Cottrell wrote in 1869:

> But to hold the doctrine of the trinity is not so much an evidence of evil intention as of intoxication from that wine of which all nations have drunk. The fact that this was one of the leading doctrines, if not the very chief, upon which the bishop of Rome was exalted to the popedom, does not say much in its favor.[30]

Although in her later writings Ellen White did endorse a "trinity", it was not the orthodox Christian doctrine she taught.[31,32] The church did not have a Trinitarian statement of belief until 1946 and today, while its Fundamental Belief No. 2 sounds correct, the church has never renounced EGW's explanation of the Trinity as "the three Dignitaries of heaven". Within Adventism is a growing resurgence of overt Arianism.

Further, the church continues to refuse to resolve the question of whether Jesus had the nature of pre- or post-fall Adam. Adventism's fatal flaw is that it did not grow from the root of the apostolic church. Rather, it grew from the heresy of Arianism. That foundation which was not built on Christ allowed the church to embrace a modern prophetess and unbiblical doctrines that obscure the gospel of grace.

---

[29] See Colleen Tinker & Geremy Graham, "Discovering the Adventist Jesus", *Proclamation!*, Volume 8, Issue 3, May and June, 2007.

[30] R.F. Cottrell, *Advent Review and Sabbath Herald,* 07-06-1869, Vol.6, No. 24, p. 185.

[31] *Journal of the Adventist Theological Society* (JATS), Spring 2006, "The Quest for a Biblical Trinity: Ellen White's 'heavenly Trio' Compared to the Traditional Doctrine," by Dr. Jerry Moon, Andrews University Theological Seminary.

[32] http://news.adventist.org/data/2007/09/1192296336/index.html.en

Chapter
THREE

Remnant Church of Bible Prophecy

Seventh-day Adventists still hold that they are the true, remnant church depicted in Revelation 12. Fundamental Belief No. 13 entitled, "Remnant and Its Mission" reads as follows:

> The universal church is composed of all who truly believe in Christ, but in the last days, a time of widespread apostasy, a remnant has been called out to keep the commandments of God and the faith of Jesus. This remnant announces the arrival of the judgment hour, proclaims salvation through Christ, and heralds the approach of His second advent. This proclamation is symbolized by the three angels of Revelation 14; it coincides with the work of judgment in heaven and results in a work of repentance and reform on earth. Every believer is called to have a personal part in this worldwide witness.

This statement is carefully worded so that it excludes from "the remnant" all but Seventh-day Adventists. No other church holds the 1844 investigative judgment hour message of SDAs. This is their unique "contribution" to Christian theology.[1]

All churches that worship on Sunday are a part of the "widespread apostasy," "Babylon" or the "daughters of Babylon". So even as SDAs acknowledge that God has His children in all churches, they add, "but through the remnant church He proclaims a message that is to restore His true worship *by calling His people out* of the apostasy and

---

[1] See *Cultic Doctrine* and *Daniel 8:14* for a thorough evaluation of this unbiblical, anti-gospel doctrine.

preparing them for Christ's return."[2] A Christian, then, is not prepared for Christ's return unless he has joined "the remnant", the Seventh-day Adventist church.

This one doctrine mandates the raiding of other churches. SDAs feel called not only to reach non-Christians, but to convert Christians to the "truths" of Adventism. Thus, their Revelation Seminars and other evangelistic programs are structured to get people—even believing evangelicals—to make a decision to join the "remnant church". Those who do are said to have finally "come into the truth."[3]

One can immediately see how difficult it is for in-formed evangelicals to work with Adventists. It is also difficult, even deceptive, for Adventists to honestly work with evangelicals.

Traditionally, Adventists have supported their claim to be the remnant church of Bible prophecy by linking their two "proof texts" of Revelation 12:17 and 19:10.

> And the dragon was enraged with the woman, and went off to make war with the rest of her offspring, who keep the commandments of God and hold to the testimony of Jesus (Rev. 12:17).

From this text they seek to "prove" that the rest (remnant, KJV) have two identification marks: (1) they keep "the commandments of God" and (2) they have the "testimony of Jesus." The commandments are interpreted to

---

[2] P.G. Damsteegt, et al., *Seventh-day Adventists Believe...A Biblical Exposition of 28 Fundamental Doctrines,* (Washington D.C.: Ministerial Association, General Conference of Seventh-day Adventists, 2005) p. 197.

[3] "Come into the truth" is a term frequently used by SDAs when speaking of other "Christians" who have accepted the teachings of Adventism.

be the Ten Commandments, including the fourth commandment of the seventh-day Sabbath.

The second identification of the remnant, Adventists
say, is "the testimony of Jesus." To explain what this
means, they immediately jump to Rev. 19:10 where they
read,

> And I fell at his feet to worship him. And he said to me, "Do
> not do that; I am a fellow servant of yours and your brethren
> who hold the testimony of Jesus; worship God. For the
> testimony of Jesus is the spirit of prophecy."

From this verse they define the testimony of Jesus as
the spirit of prophecy. So, they say, the remnant church will
keep the seventh-day Sabbath and have the "spirit of
prophecy". According to the Fundamental Beliefs of
Seventh-day Adventists, No. 18,

> One of the gifts of the Holy Spirit is prophecy. This gift is an
> *identifying mark* of the remnant church and was manifested in
> the ministry of *Ellen G. White.* As the Lord's messenger, her
> writings are *a continuing and authoritative source of truth*
> which provide for the church comfort, guidance, instruction,
> and correction...(emphasis added)

Here, right in their doctrinal statement, SDAs list the
prophetic ministry of Ellen White as "an identifying mark
of the remnant church."

The SDA claim to be the remnant church of Bible
prophecy rests, then, upon their Sabbath keeping and their
acceptance of Ellen White as "the spirit of prophecy."

Adventists fail to observe that in the writings of John,
the Greek word, *entole,* and translated "commandment" in
Revelation 12:17, is never used for the old covenant, Ten
Commandment, law. Rather John always refers to old
covenant law by the Greek word, *nomos,* translated, "law."[4]

---

[4] See Ratzlaff, *Sabbath in Christ,* p. 374–376, (LAM Publications,
LLC, PO Box 11587, Glendale, AZ 85318) for a thorough discussion

Thus, their claim that the Sabbath commandment is in view here is without warrant.

Adventists' use of Rev. 19:10 puts EGW in the place of Christ. Our Lord Jesus Christ, however, and not Ellen White, is the spirit and theme of all prophecy. Note how the following Bible translations have captured this thought.

> Those who bear testimony to Jesus are inspired like the prophets (The New English Bible).

> For the truth revealed by Jesus is the inspiration of all prophecy (Weymouth).

> For the testimony of Jesus is what inspires prophecy (Goodspeed).

> It is the truth concerning Jesus which inspires all prophecy (Knox).

> The purpose of all prophecy and of all I have shown you is to tell about Jesus (Living Bible).

> For the essence of prophecy is to give a clear witness for Jesus. (New Living Translation).

Jesus is the theme and spirit of all prophecy. This text has nothing to do with Ellen White. Jesus said,

> You search the Scriptures, because you think that in them you have eternal life; and it is these that bear witness of Me (John 5:39).

It is very clear that Adventists misuse both Revelation 12:17 and 19:10 in their claim to be the true, remnant church of Bible prophecy.

---

of this topic and a complete listing of *entole* and *nomos* in the writings of John.

FOUR

Sabbath Observance, the Seal of God

Revelation depicts a sharp demarcation between those who serve God and those who serve the "beast".[1] Adventists have traditionally held that the seventh-day Sabbath is the seal of God. Ellen White on numerous occasions confirmed this belief in her writings. She wrote that Sabbath observance would be the "line of distinction" in the "final test" that will separate God's end-time people who "receive the seal of God" and are saved, from those who "receive the mark of the beast"[2] and are cast into the lake of fire.

The traditional Adventist support for the seventh-day Sabbath as the seal of God comes from the common understanding of what a seal is. It is a mark which shows authenticity by (1) giving the name of the one in authority, (2) the title of the one in authority, and (3) the dominion of the one in authority. Seventh-day Adventists show that the Sabbath of the fourth commandment has all of this information.

This may be good human reasoning, but the New Testament never speaks of the Sabbath as the seal of God.

---

[1] Rev. 7:2, 3; 13:17; 14:9, 11; 16:2; 20:4.

[2] Ellen G. White, *The Great Controversy Between Christ and Satan*, p. 605. Describing a supposed vision direct from God, she wrote, "I saw that the Holy Sabbath *is,* and will be, the *separating wall* between the true Israel of God [in context, true SDAs] and *unbelievers*" (*Early Writings*, p. 33). She also wrote that Sabbath observance "was of sufficient importance to draw a line between *the people of God* and *unbelievers*" (Ibid., p. 85). (Emphasis added)

Because the Sabbath commandment was placed in the very center of the Ten Commandments, it served as the dynastic sign of the Sinaitic Covenant.[3] On several occasions within the old covenant we find the Sabbath called a sign. In context it is *always* the sign between God and the *sons of Israel*.[4]

Never is the Sabbath called a seal or a sign within the New Testament. Rather, the Holy Spirit is said to be the seal which the Christian receives when he believes.

> Now He who establishes us with you in Christ and anointed us in God, who also sealed us and gave us the Spirit in our hearts as a pledge (2 Cor. 1:21, 22).

> In Him, you also, after listening to the message of truth, the gospel of your salvation—having also believed, you were sealed in Him with the Holy Spirit of promise, who is given as a pledge of our inheritance, with a view to the redemption of God's own possession, to the praise of His glory (Eph. 1:13, 14).

> And do not grieve the Holy Spirit of God, by whom you were sealed for the day of redemption (Eph. 4:30).

According to Scripture it is the Holy Spirit and not the seventh-day Sabbath that is the seal of God. According to the New Testament the seventh-day Sabbath is not the sign which is to be remembered. Rather, Christians are to celebrate the Lord's Supper (the new covenant sign)[5] in remembrance of Christ.

Some Adventist evangelists now admit that the Holy Spirit is the seal but maintain that the Sabbath is the "sign of the seal", thus seeking to maintain their traditional

---

[3] See *Sabbath in Christ,* pp. 40–43, 50 and Meredith G. Kline, *Treaty of the Great King,* (Wm. B. Eerdmans Publishing Company, Grand Rapids, MI, 1963) pp. 13, 14.

[4] Ex. 31:13, 17; Ez. 20:12, 20.

[5] See Matt. 26:28; Luke 22:19, 20.

teachings and make it sound as if they agree with New Testament understanding.

There is no major problem with Christians worshiping on Saturday. However, when SDAs make their Sabbath-keeping a sign that they are right and everyone else is wrong, then that teaching becomes divisive. This is especially so when such great importance is placed on a divergent teaching. There is no command to keep the Sabbath in the New Testament. Every Sabbath meeting in the book of Acts is in a Jewish setting. It is clear that the Epistles never place positive emphasis on Sabbath keeping. Never do they explain how Gentile believers are to keep the Sabbath, and Sabbath-breaking is never included in any New Testament lists of sins.[6] This certainly seems strange if the Sabbath, as Adventists claim, is to be *the* testing truth for *all* Christians in the last days.[7] The Apostle Paul teaches that the Sabbath is to be included with the other ritual holy days of the old covenant and serves only as a shadow of Christ.[8]

By *requiring* Sabbath observance, Adventists are following the Galatian heresy—the legalistic observances of old covenant law.[9]

---

[6] See *Sabbath in Christ,* and D.A. Carson *From Sabbath to Lord's Day,* (Zondervan Publishing House, Grand Rapids, MI).

[7] "The Sabbath will be the great test of loyalty...when the final test shall be brought to bear upon men, then the line of distinction will be drawn between those who serve God and those who serve him not." *The Great Controversy,* p. 605.

[8] See Col. 2:16 and *Sabbath in Christ,* pp. 247–258.

[9] The issues in Galatia were circumcision, table fellowship with Gentiles based on Jewish food laws and observance of old covenant holy days. Adventists not only require Sabbath keeping, but also enforce the old covenant food laws of "clean" and "unclean". See "Fundamental Beliefs" No. 22.

One of the big problems for those who *require* Sabbath observance is to determine how the Sabbath is to be kept. Does one keep it by old covenant guidelines as Ellen White recommended?[10] If so, no Adventist keeps it correctly.[11] Does one keep it by the additional guidelines of Ellen White? If so they will find a huge list of legalistic rules.[12] Or, is a Sabbath-keeper to follow the 20 page list of Sabbath rules promoted by Adventist "Sabbath scholar", Samuele Bacchiocchi?[13] As is true of any *required* legalistic observance, one never knows when his observance is "good enough".

What usually happens is that each subculture of Adventism will create its own accepted norm of Sabbath observance. Then this norm is used as the standard by which to judge others. Some will not go out to eat at a restaurant on Sabbath. Others will. Some say it is permissible *if* you pay for your meal ticket on Friday. Some say that it is wrong to pay for a meal on Sabbath using cash but it is acceptable to do so when using a credit card. Some hold that it is wrong to pay for a meal on Sabbath in a secular restaurant but it is in keeping with Sabbath law to do so in an Adventist institution.[14] Some say it is fine to go swimming on Sabbath. Others say no. Some say it is permissible to wade in water on the Sabbath, but never over your knees.

---

[10] Ellen G. White, *Patriarchs and Prophets,* p. 296.

[11] See *Sabbath in Christ,* p 71–77 for a summary of biblical Sabbath laws.

[12] See *Sabbath in Christ,* p. 388–392 for a number of Sabbath rules laid down by Ellen White.

[13] Samuele Bacchiocchi, *The Sabbath in the New Testament,* (Biblical Perspectives, 4569 Lisa Lane, Berrien Springs, MI 49103), p. 211–232.

[14] The author has personally witnessed or spoken to Adventists or former Adventists who have personally witnessed all the variety of Sabbath behaviors mentioned.

Most say it is acceptable Sabbath-keeping to go for a hike as long as it is not too strenuous.

Ellen White said that parents who let their children play on the Sabbath are seen by God as Sabbath-breakers. Notice how she frames the importance of this counsel as "above every thing".

> Parents, above every thing, take care of your children upon the Sabbath. Do not suffer them to violate God's holy day by playing in the house or out of doors. You may just as well break the Sabbath yourselves as to let your children do it, and when you suffer your children to wander about, and suffer them to play upon the Sabbath, God looks upon you as Sabbath-breakers. Your children, that are under your control, should be made to mind you. Your word should be their law. Will not parents wake up to their duty before it shall be too late, and take hold of the work in earnest, redeem the time, and make unsparing efforts to save their children?
>
> 15

---

[15] *Review & Herald,* 1854-09-19.

One man regards one day above another, another regards every day alike. Let each man be fully convinced in his own mind

Chapter
FIVE

Sunday Observance, the Mark of the Beast

The flip side of Adventist's teaching that the Sabbath is the seal of God is their teaching that Sunday observance is, or will become, the mark of the beast. Remembering that the writings of Ellen G. White are "a continuing and authoritative source of truth," consider the following statement:

> The sign, or seal, of God is revealed in the observance of the seventh-day Sabbath, the Lord's memorial of creation...The mark of the beast is the opposite—the observance of the first day of the week. This mark distinguishes those who acknowledge the supremacy of the papal authority from those who acknowledge the authority of God.[1]

On one hand, Adventists want Christians to consider them to be within mainstream Christianity. On the other, SDAs condemn all Sunday-keeping mainstream churches. Many evangelicals, not knowing the real teachings of SDAs, consider them as mainstream Christians or even evangelicals. Their mainstream appearance, however, is only a façade.

The Adventist teaching that the Sabbath is the seal of God and Sunday observance is, or will become, the mark of the beast, while completely unbiblical, is one of the most effective levers Adventist preachers have in their evangelistic tool box. Coupled with other distinctive doctrines such

---

[1] *Testimonies for the Church,* Vol. 8, p. 117.

as the SDA church being the remnant church of Bible prophecy, it has tremendous emotional drawing power. Adventist evangelists quote the frightening description of those who receive the mark of the beast.

> And another angel, a third one, followed them, saying with a loud voice, "If anyone worships the beast and his image, and receives a mark on his forehead or upon his hand, he also will drink of the wine of the wrath of God, which is mixed in full strength in the cup of His anger; and he will be tormented with fire and brimstone in the presence of the holy angels and in the presence of the Lamb. And the smoke of their torment goes up forever and ever; and they have no rest day and night, those who worship the beast and his image, and whoever receives the mark of his name."[2]

Then, with this large lever of fear, they put the squeeze on those attending their Revelation Seminars and other evangelistic programs. Their appeal goes something like this: "You must come out of Babylon (Roman Catholicism) and leave the daughters of Babylon (the fallen Sunday-keeping Protestant churches) in order to avoid the mark of the beast. If you want to receive the seal of God you must begin keeping the seventh-day Sabbath and join the Seventh-day Adventist Church which is God's only true, remnant church of Bible prophecy." Thus, SDA doctrine is often the point of decision rather than faith in Jesus Christ. While SDAs do preach Christ,[3] the strong pull of their evangelism is their exclusive, unbiblical doctrines. For those who wish to leave Adventism, these doctrines are like a chain which binds them to the "true church" and makes them fearful even to visit churches that worship on Sunday.

The teaching on the mark of the beast is not some sideline teaching in Adventism, even though it is often left

---

[2] Rev. 14:9–11.

[3] It is often Christ *plus* the distinctive doctrines of Adventism.

out of their public relations or media advertising. It is central to historic Adventism. The three angels' messages found in Revelation 14:6–11 are the heart of Adventism. Of these, the third angel's message, quoted above, dealing with the mark of the beast is mentioned by Ellen White some 754 times. However, the message of the first angel, which is the gospel message, is mentioned by comparison only 121 times.[4] The term, "third angel's message" is so central to the proclamation given by Adventists, it is often used synonymously for the Adventist message.[5]

---

[4] According to the *Chosen Works* DC on the writings of Ellen White.
[5] *Testimonies for the Church,* Vol. 1, p. 208, 232, 323, 333, 486, 553.

Truly, truly, I say to you, he who hears My word, and believes Him who sent Me, has eternal life, and does not come into judgment, but has passed out of death into life.

Chapter
SIX

Judgment Started October 22, 1844

Before we consider the current Adventist teaching on this doctrine a little summary background is needed.[1]

- This doctrine continues to build on the faulty assumption that October 22, 1844, is a valid interpretation of the 2,300 days of Daniel 8:14.

- This doctrine is a *reinterpretation* of the "seventh-month movement" which predicted Christ would return to the earth on October 22, 1844; which itself was a reinterpretation of the prediction that Christ would come in 1843.

- This doctrine did *not* originate through diligent Bible study but came through a "vision" to Hiram Edson, a man who was neither known beforehand nor afterward, to manifest the true gift of prophecy.

- Edson had this "vision" October 23, 1844, the morning after Adventist's "Great Disappointment" that Christ had not come. It was a time of extreme emotional instability among the Adventists.[2]

- This doctrine is completely unknown in all of Christian history and theology.

---

[1] For a much more in-depth description and evaluation of this doctrine see Ratzlaff, *Cultic Doctrine.*

[2] "They were unable to find their bearings..." See Editor's Note in *Spirit of Prophecy,* Vol. 4, p. 499.

After receiving this "vision", Edson meet with Mr. O.L.R. Crosier who wrote out and published this new "truth". Following is a summary of their insightful "vision". It said that:

- Christ entered the Most Holy Place of the heavenly sanctuary for *the first time* on October 22, 1844.
- *No* atonement was made at the cross but atonement is made by the High Priest *in the heavenly sanctuary*.
- The blotting out of sins does *not* take place at the point of repentance and conversion.
- *The atonement is <u>not</u> complete* until Christ lays the sins of the righteous upon Satan, who is represented by the scapegoat in the Levitical Day of Atonement.[3]

Regarding this statement of "truth"—which is really heretical error—Ellen White wrote:

> The *Lord shew* [sic] *in vision*, more than one year ago, that Brother Crosier had the *true light,* on the cleansing of the Sanctuary, &c; and that it was his will, that Brother C. should write out the view which he gave us in the Day-Star, Extra, February 7, 1846. *I feel fully authorized by the Lord, to recommend that Extra to every saint.*[4] (emphasis added)

The current Adventist teaching on this doctrine is found in Fundamental Belief No. 24, "Christ's Ministry in the Heavenly Sanctuary". It describes this belief as follows:

> There is a sanctuary in heaven, the true tabernacle which the Lord set up and not man. In it Christ ministers on our behalf, making available to believers the benefits of His atoning sacrifice offered once for all on the cross. He was inaugurated as our great High Priest and began His intercessory ministry at

---

[3] For exact wording and sources see *Cultic Doctrine,* p. 97–113.
[4] *A Word to the "Little Flock",* as reproduced in Knight, *Rise of Sabbatarian Adventism,* (Review and Herald Publishing Association, Hagerstown, MD) p. 171.

the time of His ascension. In 1844, at the end of the prophetic period of 2300 days, He entered the second and last phase of His atoning ministry. It is a work of investigative judgment which is part of the ultimate disposition of all sin, typified by the cleansing of the ancient Hebrew sanctuary on the Day of Atonement. In that typical service the sanctuary was cleansed with the blood of animal sacrifices, but the heavenly things are purified with the perfect sacrifice of the blood of Jesus. The investigative judgment reveals to heavenly intelligences who among the dead are asleep in Christ and therefore, in Him, are deemed worthy to have part in the first resurrection. It also makes manifest who, among the living are abiding in Christ, keeping the commandments of God and the faith of Jesus, and in Him, therefore, are ready for translation into His everlasting kingdom. This judgment vindicates the justice of God in saving those who believe in Jesus. It declares that those who have remained loyal to God shall receive the kingdom. The completion of this ministry of Christ will mark the close of human probation before the Second Advent.

Many SDA theologians, administrators and pastors know there is no biblical support for this doctrine and many will admit to this fact in private conversation with trusted people.[5] However, this doctrine serves as the very foundation of Adventism and is strongly endorsed by Ellen White who defined Daniel 8:14 as "the central pillar of Adventism."[6] It is the glue that holds the central message of Adventism—the three angels' messages of Revelation 14—together. Many feel that to jettison this teaching would be to commit denominational suicide. After all, how can the "central pillar" of Adventism be error?

---

[5] The author has personally spoken with many SDA pastors, several SDA theologians and a few church administrators at the conference and general conference level who acknowledge this is not a biblical doctrine.
[6] *The Great Controversy*, p. 409.

The investigative judgment doctrine is like an octopus with tentacles reaching into every aspect of SDA theology.[7] Following is a summary of what is included in this doctrine. Those who want more detail with the supporting references quoted and not just listed, may find these in *Cultic Doctrine* in the chapter entitled, "The Sliver".

The Seventh-day Adventist doctrine of the cleansing of the heavenly sanctuary and the investigative judgment teaches that at His ascension Christ entered the outer apartment of the heavenly sanctuary. From that time until 1844 He performed a ministry of intercession and forgiveness analogous to that of the earthly sanctuary's outer apartment,[8] where forgiveness was only provisional and believers were not entirely freed from the condemnation of the law.[9] In 1844 Christ entered into the Most Holy Place of the heavenly sanctuary for the first time[10,11] to begin a work of investigative judgment.[12] This judgment deals only

---

[7] *Cultic Doctrine,* See the chapter entitled, "The Pillar—The Heart of SDA Theology."

[8] *The Great Controversy,* p. 420. See also *Early Writings,* p. 252; *Review and Herald,* 1850-03-01; 1905-11-09; *Spiritual Gifts,* Vol. 1, p. 158.

[9] *Patriarchs and Prophets,* p.355. See also Chris Badenhorst, "The Investigative Judgment: Your Questions Finally Answered," *Proclamation!,* http://lifeassuanceministries.org/Proclamation2005_MarApr.pdf

[10] See Knight, *Rise of Sabbatarian Adventism,* (Review and Herald Publishing Association, Hagerstown, MD), p. 126; *The Great Controversy,* p. 422; Ellen G. White, *Southern Watchman* 1905-01-24.

[11] Some Adventists make yet *another* reinterpretation in trying to harmonize EGW's statement that Christ entered into the Most Holy Place in 1844 with the teaching of Hebrews 6:19. They state that Christ entered the Most Holy Place at His ascension to dedicate the Most Holy Place and then withdrew to the Holy Place until 1844.

[12] *Review and Herald,* 1887-03-22; Ellen G. White, *Spirit of Prophecy,* Vol. 4, p. 308.

with those who have professed to believe in God.[13] The wicked, according to SDA theology, will be investigated during the 1000 years[14] and executed shortly after the close of the 1000 years of Revelation 20.[15] The investigative judgment starts with the cases of the dead, reaching clear back to Adam, and reviews the life records of every person who has professed faith in God. Every deed is closely examined. Each succeeding generation is investigated and judged.[16] At some time—none know when—the cases of the dead are completed and God then moves to the cases of the living.[17] SDAs believe they will not know when their name comes up in judgment.[18] Therefore, it is extremely important that they engage in no frivolous activity or sin. Every sin must be confessed. Sins which have been forgotten and unconfessed will stand against them in the judgment.[19] Their characters must demonstrate perfect obedience to the Ten Commandments,[20] especially the fourth commandment.[21] Some names in this list of professed believers will be accepted, others will be rejected.[22] When every person confessing faith in God has come up in review, Jesus *then* pleads his blood before the Father on behalf of those who are *found worthy,* and *then* blots out the record of their sins from the books of

---

[13] *The Great Controversy,* p. 483, 486; *Spirit of Prophecy,* Vol. 4, p. 420.

[14] *The Great Controversy,* p. 480; *Early Writings,* p. 292.

[15] *The Great Controversy,* p. 662.

[16] Ibid., p. 483.

[17] Ibid., p. 490.

[18] *Spirit of Prophecy,* Vol. 4, p. 315.

[19] *Spiritual Gifts,* Vol. 3, p. 331.

[20] *Testimonies for the Church,* Vol. 4, p. 218.

[21] *Spirit of Prophecy,* Vol. 4, p. 257; *The Great Controversy,* p. 605.

[22] Ibid., p. 483.

heaven.[23] After that, not knowing if, or when, the work of investigative judgment has been completed, the righteous, still in their human state before the second coming of Christ, will have to live in the sight of a holy God *without an intercessor*.[24] Next, *Jesus takes the sins of God's people and transfers them to Satan,* who, Adventists teach, is represented by the Day of Atonement scapegoat in Leviticus 16.[25] *Satan then bears the sins* he has caused the righteous to commit. *He will suffer for the sins of the righteous* and his own sins in the lake of fire and then be *blotted from existence*.[26] This completes the atonement.[27] The investigative judgment is conducted before all the intelligences of the universe. This vindicates the character of God before all the "unfallen beings".[28] At that time everyone will know the immutability of the law of God and the righteous character of God.[29]

This doctrine rests upon some twenty-two linking assumptions. Most of these are contrary to biblical evidence.[30] Not only is this doctrine unbiblical, its teachings are contrary to the New Testament gospel of grace.[31] Remember, this "work of judgment in heaven" judges believers by their *works,* and "every believer" is called to have a personal part in this worldwide witness—the SDA church. Carried to its logical conclusion, SDA theology

---

[23] Ibid., p. 486. See also *Spirit of Prophecy,* Vol. 4, p. 266; *Testimonies for the Church,* Vol. 3, p. 530.

[24] *Spirit of Prophecy,* Vol. 4, p. 432; *Early Writings*, p. 280; *Spiritual Gifts,* Vol. 1, p. 198; *The Great Controversy,* p. 614.

[25] Ibid., p. 422; *Spirit of Prophecy,* Vol. 4, p. 266.

[26] Ibid., p. 267.

[27] *The Great Controversy,* p. 422.

[28] *Adult Sabbath School Lessons,* 1996, "Three Angels' Messages", p. 47.

[29] White, *Review and Herald,* 1901-06-18.

[30] See *Daniel 8:14,* p. 174–176; *Cultic Doctrine,* p. 167–182.

[31] See *Cultic Doctrine,* p. 205–223.

teaches that no "believer" who failed to heed the call to join the "remnant" church and participate in its witness could legitimately expect to pass this judgment.

Adventists teach that only those who have professed to believe in God are judged in this investigative judgment. However, the Bible teaches that true believers do not come into judgment.

> Truly, truly, I say to you, he who hears My word, and believes Him who sent Me, has eternal life, and does not come into judgment, but has passed out of death into life (Jn. 5:24).

This contrary-to-the-gospel, unbiblical teaching was founded on a reinterpretation, of a reinterpretation, of a failed prophecy. The failed prophecy itself was founded on an obscure, out of context, apocalyptic passage using wild proof texting. Those who accept this doctrine as originally taught are placed under guilt, uncertainty and fear.[32] Yet the SDA church will not publically renounce it because it is "the central pillar of Adventism". Today Adventist leaders are attempting to reinterpret this outlandish doctrine *again*. Note the flip/ flop, context-hopping, "reasoning" below.

> ...We stand on their [SDA pioneers] brave and inspiring shoulders now, and *without altering a single plank of the basic pillars of faith,* we do indeed perceive a clearer vision.... Perhaps a better way, then, of expressing the *same* truth that came to Hiram Edson on that tear-filled morning would be as follows: At the Ascension, Christ went into the presence of God (and in saying this, we are in line with the New Testament) and there commenced a "first-apartment ministry" (in line with the ancient typical service). At the end of the 2300 days (years) in 1844 (in line with the book of Daniel), He commenced a "second-apartment ministry" (in line with

---

[32] The author has received hundreds of letters from former Adventists who have expressed the fear and trauma it caused them by believing this doctrine. They also expressed the joy of understanding the simple gospel of faith in Christ when they left Adventism.

the ancient typical service on the Day of Atonement)—
namely, the restoration or vindication or cleansing of the
heavenly sanctuary (in line with Leviticus 16 and Daniel
8:14). [33] (Adams' emphasis)

One Adventist Pioneer, A. F. Ballenger, quotes Elder
Spicer, another leading Adventist, showing that these
Adventist leaders knew the lack of support for the
Adventist sanctuary theology.

When I used to give Bible readings in the earlier days in
London, and took the people through the eighth of Daniel, I
always skipped hastily over those texts where we made the
sanctuary one minute in heaven and the next on earth, and the
host one time the angels and the next the pagans, and I skipped
over the statement that the taking away of the "daily" meant
the taking away of paganism by suggesting the rendering in
the original was a bit obscure so that the translation was
difficult. That is what we used to be taught in the Bible school
in Battle Creek in the old days. And all that was making no
particular use of that particular portion of Scripture. It was
simply passing over it to get down to the cleansing of the
sanctuary..." [34]

After studying this doctrine with Adventist scholars, the
late Dr. Donald Grey Barnhouse, editor of *Eternity* wrote
this:

The [sanctuary] doctrine is, to me, the most colossal, psycho-
logical, face-saving phenomenon in religious history...We
personally do not believe that there is even a suspicion of a
verse in Scripture to sustain such a peculiar position, and we
further believe that any effort to establish it is stale, flat, and
unprofitable...[it is] unimportant and almost naive. [35]

---

[33] Roy Adams, *The Sanctuary, Understanding the Heart of Adventist
Theology* (Hagerstown MD: Review and Herald Publishing Association, 1993) p. 106, 107.

[34] Bert Haloviak, 66 page paper on A. F. Ballenger, p. 45 in my loose-
leaf copy.

[35] *Eternity*, 7:67, Sept. 1956, p. 6, 7, 43–45.

Chapter
SEVEN

Promote *The Clear Word*

The Adventist church does not want to own officially *The Clear Word* "Bible", (TCW) but it is nevertheless a work of its hands. It was written by Dr. Jack J. Blanco when he was the chair of the Religion Department of Southern Adventist University. It was printed by the denominationally owned Review and Herald Publishing Association, it is promoted in Adventist journals, including their Adult Sabbath School Lessons[1] and it is sold in Adventist book centers.

My copy, which I purchased some years ago, titles this work as *The Clear Word Bible*. It is now titled *The Clear Word*. My copy has a jacket on it with the following statements. I have italicized and/or bolded key phrases which, as you continue to study this section, you will see are designed to **deceive** the reader into thinking this is an accurate rendering of God's Word in modern English.

> For everyone who hungers for a *clearer understanding of God's Word* and a richer devotional life....Imagine how much more you would get out of the Bible if the meaning of *every passage was crystal clear*...*The Clear Word Bible lets the power of ancient texts come through today*...The result of this *careful* paraphrasing is that you find not only *more understanding* in reading the Bible, you find more joy. *As the*

---

[1] There is a full-page advertisement for *The Clear Word* in the third quarter, 2006, *Adult Sabbath School Bible Study Guide* which is copyrighted by the General Conference of Seventh-day Adventists. See: http://www.absg.adventist.org/Archives.htm

meaning of Scripture becomes more transparent...every text is
*phrased to make its **original meaning as plain as possible** to a*
modern reader.

As I write this I went to the Review and Herald's web
site[2] and searched for "Bibles". It yielded fifteen different
bindings or editions including, *The Clear Word Giant
Print, The Clear Word for Kids, The Easy English Clear
Word, The Clear Word Psalms and Proverbs,* three
bindings of *The Clear Word Gospel of John, Pocket Size*
and several other editions of *The Clear Word,* including
three black, leather bindings with gilded pages, *The Clear
Word New Testament,* an audio CD read by Lonnie
Melashenko (the speaker for the Voice of Prophecy) and
the site indicated that an audio CD of *The Clear Word
Old Testament* is in the process of development.

I noticed that the descriptions of *The Clear Word* today
remain very much like the words on the jacket of *The Clear
Word Bible* I purchased some years ago. Here is the
advertising copy for *The Easy English Clear Word:*

> At Last God Speaks Your Language. What better way to get
> acquainted with the English language than to study the world's
> greatest book—the Book upon which the culture was founded.
> This fresh, slightly condensed paraphrase of the Bible conveys
> the ideas of each Bible verse in the most basic terms. There
> are no strange idioms, archaic jargon, or big words for
> scholars. Just pure, simple English to make God's message
> plain to those who are not native speakers of the language.[3]

This very morning as I am writing this, I received a
phone call from a person who lives in Canada who is
studying with an Adventist pastor. He told me that this
SDA pastor gave him *The Clear Word* for their Bible
study.

---

[2] http://www.reviewandherald.org
[3] Ibid.

Could it be that the Adventist church does not want to call *The Clear Word* an "Adventist Bible" for fear of being exposed as a cult? Could it be, however, it does want its members, including children, the aged, converts in third-world countries who do not read English well, and even evangelistic interests to read and listen to it on CDs? *The Clear Word* twists the wording of the Bible so that it agrees with the unbiblical teachings of Adventism and Ellen White. In so doing, readers of *The Clear Word* should make "good Adventists" who will remain loyal to the denomination, believing its teachings are founded on the Bible.

Many believe *The Clear Word* to be *the* most, corrupt and twisted "Bible" ever printed by a so-called Christian organization.

The lengths to which Adventists will go to find support for their sanctuary theology as outlined in the previous section are amazing. For example, *The Clear Word,* without *any manuscript support whatever,* at Daniel 8:14, reads SDA theology right into the text inside the quotes from the angel. Following is this text quoted from the NASB and then from *The Clear Word* (TCW). I have italicized and/or bolded key words and phrases that have been added, subtracted or twisted to make the text line up with Adventist theology in this and the following selection of comparisons.

> NASB: And he said to me, "For 2,300 evenings and mornings; then the holy place will be properly restored."

> TCW: He said to him, "After two thousand three hundred **prophetic days** (or **two thousand three hundred years**), God will step in, proclaim the truth about Himself and restore the ministry of the **Sanctuary in heaven** to its rightful place. This is when the **judgment will begin, of which the cleansing of the earthly sanctuary was a type**" (Parentheses shown are in the text of *The Clear Word*.)

Following are a few more illustrations which show how this "Bible" corrupts the Word of God.

> NASB: Deut. 14:26, You may spend the money for whatever your heart desires: for oxen, or sheep, or wine, or strong drink, or whatever your heart desires; and there you shall eat in the presence of the LORD your God and rejoice, you and your household.

> CWB: Deut. 14:26, When you get there buy what you want to eat and drink, whether it's beef, lamb, **unfermented** wine, or anything else that the Lord approves. (Adds "unfermented" and leaves out "strong drink", adds "anything else that the Lord *approves*".)

> NASB: 1 Cor. 10:27, If one of the unbelievers invites you and you want to go, eat anything that is set before you without asking questions for conscience' sake.

> TCW: 1 Cor. 10:27, If unbelievers invite you out to dinner and you want to go, go ahead, Whatever they serve you, **select what you can eat** and don't worry about whether it was offered to idols or not. (Changes, "eat anything that is set before you" to "select what you *can* eat", thus allowing for the continuation of "clean" and "unclean" in violation of Acts 10, 11; Rom. 14; Mk. 7:19.)

> NASB: Lk. 23:43, And He said to him, "Truly I say to you, today you shall be with Me in Paradise."

> TCW: Lk. 23:43, Jesus turned His head toward him and said, "I promise you today, **when I return with the glory of my Father**, I'll take you home with me to paradise." (Allows for soul sleep.)

> NASB: Rom. 5:10, For if while we were enemies we were reconciled to God through the death of His Son, much more, having been reconciled, we shall be saved by His life.

> TCW: Rom. 5:10, If God loved us so much that He sent His Son to die for us while we were His enemies, how much more eager God must be **to save us from evil** through His resurrected Son now that we are His friends? (Omits, "saved by **His life**".)

NASB: Gal. 4:10, 11, You observe days and months and seasons and years. I fear for you, that perhaps I have labored over you in vain. (This most likely refers to Sabbath days, new moon celebrations, annual feasts, sabbatical years.)[4]

TCW: Gal. 4:10, 11, You put a saving significance on observing all kinds of **religious holidays**, months, seasons and years. (Changes "days" to "religious holidays", removing the possibility that the Sabbath is in view.)

NASB: Col. 2:16, Therefore let no one act as your judge in regard to food or drink or in respect to a festival or a new moon or a Sabbath day.

TCW: Col. 2:16, Don't let anyone control your life by giving you a set of **ceremonial rules** about what to eat, what to drink and what monthly festivals or **special Sabbaths** to keep. (Adds "ceremonial rules" and changes Sabbath day to "special Sabbaths" thus removing the possibility that the Seventh-day Sabbath could be in view.)

NASB: Phil. 1:23, But I am hard-pressed from both directions, having the desire to depart and be with Christ, for that is very much better.

TCW: Phil 1:23, So I've been wrestling with mixed emotions. On one hand, I would prefer to be sentenced to death and in the **next moment of consciousness** see Christ, which would be much better than staying here in this old world. (Adds "next moment of consciousness" allowing for soul sleep.)

NASB: Mt. 10:28, And do not fear those who kill the body, but are unable to kill the soul; but rather fear Him who is able to destroy both soul and body in hell.

TCW: Mt. 10:28, Don't be afraid that you might be killed. They can kill your body but not your **spirit** or your loyalty to me. Now if there is something to be concerned about, **it's that you don't lose faith in God.** (Changes soul to spirit which are different Greek words, deletes "able to destroy both soul and body in hell", changes "hell" to "don't lose faith in God".)

---

[4] See R.C.H. Lenski, *Commentary on the New Testament, Galatians,* p. 213, 214; Frank E. Gaebelein, *The Expositor's Bible Commentary,* Vol. 10, p. 476; John Calvin, *Calvin's Commentary,* Vol. XXI, p. 124, 125.

NASB: Heb. 4:4, For He has thus said somewhere concerning the seventh day, "And God rested on the seventh day from all His works."

TCW: Heb. 4:4, That's why **at creation** He gave man the seventh-day **Sabbath**, not only as a reminder of **creation week**, but also as a symbol of spiritual rest. According to the Scriptures, God Himself rested on the seventh day and enjoyed this special time with man. (Makes the Sabbath a creation ordinance, makes the days of creation a "week" even though creation was finished on the 6th day.)

NASB: Jn. 10:30–33, I and the Father are one. The Jews picked up stones again to stone Him. Jesus answered them, "I showed you many good works from the Father; for which of them are you stoning Me?" The Jews answered Him, "For a good work we do not stone You, but for blasphemy; and because You, being a man, make Yourself out *to be* God."

TCW: Jn. 10:30–33, You see, my Father and I **are so close,** we're one. Then the Jewish leaders left **Solomon's Porch** and went searching for stones to kill Him, as they had before. When they came back, Jesus faced them and said, "I have done nothing but good to people, and I did all this under the direction of my Father. For which of these good works are you going to stone me?" They said, "We're not going to stone you because of the good you've done, but for blasphemy. You're only a human being, yet you keep calling yourself the **Son of God**." (A careful reading of these two verses shows its subtle deception. *The Clear Word,* by adding "are so close..." implies that the "oneness" with the Father is the oneness of a close, working relationship, where the NASB indicates the oneness is one in essence. Note also that the Jews clearly understood what Jesus was saying. "You make yourself out to be God". TCW changes this to "you keep calling your self the '*Son* of God'" thereby diminishing Christ's full deity and allowing for Arianism.)

NASB: 2 Pet. 1:1, Simon Peter, a bond-servant and apostle of Jesus Christ, to those who have received a faith of the same kind as ours, by the righteousness of our God and Savior, Jesus Christ. (Greek syntax indicates that "our God and

Savior" is the *same* person as Jesus Christ showing Christ's full deity.)[5]

TCW: 2 Pet. 1:1, This letter is from Peter, a servant and apostle of Jesus Christ, to those who have received the same precious faith as we have, the good news about what God has done for us **through** our Savior Jesus Christ. (Makes "God" and "our Savior Jesus Christ" separate persons allowing for Arianism.)

NASB: Jude 9, But Michael the archangel, when he disputed with the devil and argued about the body of Moses, did not dare pronounce against him a railing judgment, but said, "The Lord rebuke you."

TCW: Jude 9, In contrast to these ungodly men is the **Lord Jesus Christ, also called Michael, the archangel** in charge of the entire angelic host. When He was challenged by Satan about His intentions to resurrect Moses, He didn't come at Satan with a blistering attack nor did he belittle him. He simply said, "God rejects your claim to his body." (Adds "the Lord Jesus Christ" and makes Christ, Michael the archangel in harmony with early Adventist teachings and the writings of Ellen White.)[6]

NASB: Rev. 1:10, I was in the Spirit on the Lord's day, and I heard behind me a loud voice like the sound of a trumpet.

TCW: Rev. 1:10, One **Sabbath morning** when I had gone to the rocky island shore to **meditate and worship**, I suddenly heard a voice behind me that sounded as loud as a trumpet." (Omits "I was in the Spirit", changes "Lord's day"[7] to "Sabbath morning", adds "to meditate and worship".)

There are literally hundreds of such corruptions in *The Clear Word*.[8] This is serious error. The Bible is replete with commands NOT to alter the Word of God.

---

[5] R.C.H. Lenski, *Commentary on the New Testament,* 2 Peter, p. 252.
[6] *Testimonies for the Church,* Vol. 3, p. 220.
[7] The Lord's Day was a common designation for Sunday in the early church. See D.A. Carson, *From Sabbath to Lord's Day,* p. 221–250.
[8] See Dr. Verle Streifling's paper on *The Clear Word* for many more illustrations at www.lifeassuranceministries.com/art.html

> You shall not add to the word which I am commanding you, nor take away from it, that you may keep the commandments of the LORD your God which I command you (Deut. 4:2).

> Every word of God is tested; He is a shield to those who take refuge in Him. Do not add to His words lest He reprove you, and you be proved a liar (Prov. 30:5, 6).

> ...Scripture cannot be broken (Jn. 10:35).

> Sanctify them in the truth; Your word is truth (Jn. 17:17).

> I testify to everyone who hears the words of the prophecy of this book: if anyone adds to them, God shall add to him the plagues which are written in this book; and if anyone takes away from the words of the book of this prophecy, God shall take away his part from the tree of life and from the holy city, which are written in this book" (Rev. 22:18, 19).

God's Word is true, therefore, changing it results in lies and error. What honest Christian would want to change God's Word? What true Christian church would allow for such deception? None!

The Clear Word manufactures support for Adventist's sanctuary theology, abstaining from the use of wine or strong drink, required Sabbath observance in the new covenant and continued enforcement of clean and unclean meats. It compromises the biblical teachings of the days of creation, the nature of man in death as the separation of body and spirit, deletes hell, distorts the gospel of Christ and substitutes the Sabbath for the Lord's Day.

If the above corruptions were not enough, *The Clear Word* equates Jesus with Michael the archangel and compromises the full deity of Christ some 27 times.[9] This is no little matter to be swept under the denominational rug. The full deity of Christ is a cardinal doctrine of the Christian

---

[9] http://www.lifeassuranceministries.com/art.html, then click on "SDAs Corrupt Clear Word Bible".

church. To reject the full, eternal, deity of Christ is one of the chief characteristics of a cult. While SDAs Fundamental Beliefs statement on the nature of Christ may be correct, the fact that the SDA church continues to promote this corrupt "Bible" shows the far-reaching subtle deception that is still present in this organization.

The title page of *The Clear Word* states that it is:

> An expanded paraphrase of the Bible to nurture faith and growth.

Doubtless *The Clear Word* will nurture faith and growth in the "Adventist message", but certainly not in the apostolic faith that was once and for all delivered to the saints.[10]

Could it be that Dr. Jack J. Blanco has such faith in the writings of Ellen G. White as a continuing and authoritative *source* of truth that he actually believes his work is the way God wants it and thinks *The Clear Word* is actually an improvement on the Bible? Could it be that the reason there is no wide-spread outcry among the membership of the Adventist church *demanding* this work be removed is because many see no error therein? Could it be this is the end result of holding the writings of Ellen White as an authoritative *source* of truth and as an *inspired commentary* on the Bible?

Many Adventists believe that the Writings of Ellen White are "an *inspired* commentary" on the Bible. An illustration of this is the large King James Version "Study Bible" which is also printed by the Review and Herald Publishing Association and sold in Adventist bookstores. In it are hundreds if not thousands of references to the writings of Ellen White. These are listed in marginal columns often with key statements by Ellen White printed

---

[10] Jud. 1:3.

below the Bible text. On the introductory page, "About the Study Bible", we find these words.

> But God in his goodness has once again caused "the testimony of Christ" to be confirmed in his church, so that we "come behind in no gift; waiting for the coming of the Lord Jesus Christ" (1 Cor. 1:6-7). His last day remnant people have had restored through the ministry of Ellen G. White, "the testimony of Jesus" which is "the spirit of prophecy" (Rev. 12:17, 19:10). *To combine this **inspired commentary** with the Scriptures themselves is the purpose of this present volume.* It is the heartfelt and earnest prayer of the publishers, that this inspired Word, with its accompanying **inspired commentary,** will go out into all the world and prepare a people for the great day of God." (emphasis added)

The only conceivable rational for the writing and continued promotion of *The Clear Word* is the acceptance of the writings of Ellen White as "a continuing and authoritative *source of truth*" *and* as "an **inspired** commentary of the Bible".

Purposeful changing of the biblical text in *The Clear Word* to support the unbiblical doctrines of the SDA church and Ellen G. White is inexcusable. These changes have been made without *any* manuscript support, often in violation of Hebrew or Greek syntax and the accepted definition of Hebrew or Greek words. This was done by one who was the chair of the Religion Department at a leading Adventist University, who holds a Doctorate of Theology in New Testament. Considering what was written on the jacket of my copy of *The Clear Word Bible* as presented above, this must be seen for what it is: *purposeful, blatant, deception of the worst kind.* This is something *only* a cult would do when either: (1) it knows that its teachings cannot be supported by honest contextual study using a legitimate Bible; or (2) it actually believes *The Clear Word* is an improvement on the Bible based upon Adventist's other *source* of truth—the *inspired commentary* of Ellen White.

Chapter
EIGHT

Dead Persons No Longer Exist

The Adventist teaching of soul sleep is set forth in the Fundamental Belief No. 26, "Death and Resurrection" as follows:

> The wages of sin is death. But God, who alone is immortal, will grant eternal life to His redeemed. Until that day death is an unconscious state for all people. When Christ, who is our life, appears, the resurrected righteous and the living righteous will be glorified and caught up to meet their Lord. The second resurrection, the resurrection of the unrighteous, will take place a thousand years later.

Most evangelicals believe the spirits of deceased Christians go immediately "to be with the Lord."[1] Then they are reunited with a resurrected body at the second coming of Christ.[2] Adventists interpret the "spirit" to be only breath. They teach that a "soul" is a living person with body *and* breath. Adventists, like Jehovah's Witnesses, say that in death the souls are sleeping—actually don't really exist—until the bodily resurrection.

In the book, *Seventh-day Adventists Believe,* under the heading "The Person Returns to Dust," a "person" is said to be an "organic unity" in which "body and soul only exist together; they form an indivisible union."[3] The "soul" is not

---

[1] See 2 Cor. 5:1–10; Phil. 1:21–26; 2 Tim. 1:10; Mark 12:18–27; Jn. 6:40, 47; Jn. 8:51; Jn. 11:25, 26.

[2] See 1 Cor. 15:35–58; 1 Thess. 4:13–18.

[3] P. 391.

an entity having an individual self-conscious identity. It is nothing more than "breath," or "the life principle."[4] Its return to God is nothing more than God withdrawing the power of life. The lifeless body, which is no longer a "person", then disintegrates in the grave. SDA doctrine therefore denies that any real "person" exists between death and resurrection.

This creates a philosophical and ontological problem for Seventh-day Adventism. Clearly, according to such doctrine, in death a person ceases to exist. And if a person ceases to exist at death, then "resurrection" can have nothing to do with the person who died but will be the creation of another being altogether. Even if, at the resurrection, God were to install all the memories, thought patterns, even DNA structure, of such a previously existing person, it is still a new, different being. Of what interest can such a being be to one who knows his own existence will certainly come to a complete end at death?

Perhaps to counter this problem and the hopeless despair it necessarily entails, SDAs offer this statement:

> Death is not complete annihilation; it is only a state of temporary unconsciousness while the person awaits the resurrection.[5]

The statement that, "death is not complete annihilation," is disingenuous. It is not "complete" annihilation, in SDA thinking, because it is not final, but only "temporary." But annihilation is final, and therefore complete, by definition. "Incomplete annihilation" is an oxymoron. To say, "the person awaits the resurrection," is equally disingenuous. According to their own definitions there is no "person" between death and the resurrection. Awaiting

---

[4] Ibid., p. 353.
[5] Ibid., p. 352

implies anticipation. Anticipation is a function of consciousness requiring a conscious existence. Both are impossible during death according to SDA doctrine. No dead thing "awaits" anything.

If "a person" ends at death there can be no such thing as "eternal life" for persons who die. Those persons are gone, period. This is not the teaching of the New Testament. Jesus said,

> Truly, truly, I say to you, he who believes *has* eternal life (Jn. 6:47).

In Greek, "has" is present, indicative active, indicating eternal life is a *present reality*. Paul said,

> Therefore, being always of good courage, and knowing that while we are at home in the body we are absent from the Lord—for we walk by faith, not by sight—we are of good courage, I say, and prefer rather to be absent from the body and to be at home with the Lord. Therefore also we have as our ambition, whether at home or absent, to be pleasing to Him (2 Cor. 5:6–9).

These statements show that the Christian now has eternal life and at death his spirit is going to be present with the Lord. Further, in the intermediate state there is consciousness as one can be "pleasing to the Lord" when absent from the body.

The Bible teaches that mankind is body, soul *and* spirit[6] and our "spirit" is more than just breath. When we are "born again", our spirits are reborn.[7] We become new creatures and the Holy Spirit communicates with our spirit.

> The Spirit Himself bears witness with our spirit that we are children of God (Rom. 8:16).

---

[6] 1 Thess. 5:23; Heb. 4:12.
[7] Jn. 3:5–8.

Thus at death our spirits depart to be with Christ, and at the resurrection, they are reunited with new bodies; but all the while we exist because we *now* have eternal life.

Typical of Adventist teaching, those who disagree with their understanding and teaching are said to be deceived by Satan. Ellen White stated that,

> Through the two great errors, the immortality of the soul and Sunday sacredness, Satan will bring the people under his deceptions. While the former lays the foundation of spiritualism, the latter creates a bond of sympathy with Rome. The Protestants of the United States will be foremost in stretching their hands across the gulf to grasp the hand of spiritualism; they will reach over the abyss to clasp hands with the Roman power; and under the influence of this threefold union, this country will follow in the steps of Rome in trampling on the rights of conscience.[8]

Ellen White teaches that Christians who believe that at death the human spirit "goes to be with the Lord" are deceived by Satan.

---

[8] *The Great Controversy,* p. 588. See also *Spirit of Prophecy,* Vol. 4, p. 405.

Chapter
NINE

Gospel Additions

There are two formulas that are suggested for salvation. One is the basic Christian formula. The other is the one often promoted by the cults:

Faith in Christ = Salvation + Good Works
> or
Faith in Christ + Good Works = Salvation

In Ephesians 2:8–10, Paul explains that salvation is a gift of God based on faith. But even the faith itself comes from God. Then, after salvation comes good works. Why are people saved by God's unmerited grace? One reason, Paul says, is to do good works. Salvation results in us becoming new creatures in Christ "unto good works." Christians will do good works, not because they must do so to gain salvation, but now that they have been saved, they are new creatures in Christ,[1] and it is their nature to do good works in response to God's grace. Hence, the first formula is biblical.

However, it is the second formula that the cults will always use. They will place works before salvation. What works? Each group will have its own unique list that must

---

[1] 2 Cor. 5:17.

be followed to the letter of the law, or salvation is out of reach.[2]

Following are summaries of the teachings of Ellen White, whose writings are "a continuing and authoritative *source* of truth."

She said that William Miller's 1843 date-setting, second-coming message was a "saving message" and pastors who resisted this message had "the blood of souls" upon them.[3] Faith in Christ was not enough. They had to add to their faith the "good work" of date setting.

Churches that rejected the revised 1844 sanctuary "truth" fell from God's favor and became "Babylon" even though they continued to have faith in Christ. She said that the people in these churches were deceived by Satan, and their prayers were useless.[4]

Ellen White said that Christians should never say "I am saved."[5] She said that only those who keep the seventh-day

---

[2] See Rick Branch, "Profile, Patterns In The Cults," in *Watchman Expositor,* Vol. 11, No. 2, 1994.

[3] *Early Writings,* p. 243.

[4] *Spiritual Gifts,* Vol. 1, p. 140, 172, 173.

[5] "We are *never* to rest in a satisfied condition, and cease to make advancement, saying, '*I am saved.*' When this idea is entertained, the motives for watchfulness, for prayer, for earnest endeavor to press onward to higher attainments, cease to exist. *No sanctified tongue will be found uttering these words till Christ shall come, and we enter in through the gates into the city of God."* White, *The Kress Collection,* p. 120. The important thing is *why* EGW said this. *"No man can say, I am saved, until he has endured test and trial, until he has shown that he can overcome temptation."* *Review and Herald,* 1890-06-17. EGW taught that only those who had *proven* they could overcome temptation could lay claim to salvation. And then she put this out of the reach of all by saying that assurance of salvation could only be obtained *after* the second coming. (all emphases added)

Sabbath will be saved in the last days.[6] She taught that there will be no change in character at the second coming.[7]

She said we are not saved by faith alone.[8] She said we must live a life of "perfect obedience" *before* God's promises will be fulfilled to us.[9]

While some SDAs reject this theology, it is nonetheless Adventist teaching endorsed by their "messenger of God," Ellen White.

Most Adventists have little assurance of salvation. Many cannot tell you when they were born again, if, indeed they were.

---

[6] Ellen G. White, *Medical Ministry,* p. 123.

[7] White, *Review and Herald,* 1892-06-21.

[8] "Faith and works are the two oars with which we are to make our way in the Christian life. The Lord calls upon all who think they know what faith is, to be sure that they are not pulling with only one oar, and their little bark [boat] going round and round, making no progress at all. Faith without intelligent works is dead. *Faith in the healing power of God will not save unless it is combined with good works."* Ellen G. White, *Australasian Union Record,* 1905-10-15. "It is Satan's studied effort to divert the minds of men from the one way of salvation,—faith in Christ, *and* obedience to the law of God." Ellen G. White, *Sketches from the Life of Paul,* p. 192.

[9] "*If* we live a life of *perfect obedience,* His promises will be fulfilled toward us." *Testimonies for the Church,* Vol. 2, p. 122. "What God promises He is able at any time to perform, and the work which He gives His people to do He is able to accomplish by them. If they will live according to every word He has spoken, every good word and promise will be fulfilled unto them. But *if they come short of perfect obedience, the great and precious promises are afar off, and they cannot reach the fulfillment."* *Testimonies for the Church,* Vol. 2, p. 148. (all above emphases added)

If we say that we have fellowship with Him and yet walk in the darkness, we lie and do not practice the truth.

Chapter
TEN

Deceptive Practices Sill Used

Often evangelicals base their inclusion of the Adventist Church within mainstream Christianity upon Walter Martin's evaluation in *Kingdom of the Cults*.[1] What many do not know is that the book, *Questions on Doctrine,*[2] which was written to persuade Walter Martin and Donald Grey Barnhouse of the evangelical nature of Adventism, was soon rejected by many Adventist leaders and laity alike and was allowed to go out of print. At the time *Questions on Doctrine* was written, Andrews University Seminary was controlled by evangelical leaning Adventists. However, shortly thereafter a big shake up occurred and the Seminary was then controlled by historic Adventists who moved Adventism back toward its cultic past.

Shortly before his death, Walter Martin was a guest on the John Ankerberg show along with William Johnson, the editor of the Adventist Review. It is clear by this interview that Walter Martin saw the Adventist church slipping back into its cultic past.

It is evident that SDAs hold some unique, unbiblical teachings that are quite divergent from mainstream Christianity. However, Adventists do not want to appear to be that divergent! Rather, they want to be seen by Christen-

---

[1] Walter Martin, *Kingdom of the Cults,* (Bethany House, 1965).
[2] *Questions on Doctrine,* Prepared by a Representative Group of Seventh-day Adventist Leaders, Bible Teachers and Editors, (Review and Herald Publishing Association, Washington, D.C., 1956).

dom as within the mainstream. In order to do this, they have become very subtle in their evangelism. Seldom are their Revelation Seminars and Bible lectures advertised as Adventist evangelistic meetings. The Voice of Prophecy, Faith for Today, It Is Written, The Quiet Hour, Amazing Facts, 3ABN and other SDA media programs are often not advertised as Adventist programs. These programs often leave out of their messages some of the erroneous doctrines outlined in this booklet. First, they want to "set the hook", and then after they have the "fish in the boat," they tell them "the rest of the story." The author has spoken with many Seventh-day Adventists or former Seventh-day Adventists who were never told about all the unbiblical doctrines, including the acceptance of Ellen White as a continuing and authoritative source of truth, until after they were baptized into the church.[3] Most know nothing of the

---

[3] At the SDA General Conference held in Toronto, Canada in June/July, 2000, a revised Baptismal Certificate and accompanying vow was adopted. If this new procedure is followed, everyone joining the SDA church should be aware of Adventist doctrine. The new instructions read: "Candidates for baptism or those being received into fellowship by profession of faith shall affirm their acceptance of the doctrinal beliefs of the Seventh-day Adventist Church in the presence of the church or other properly appointed body. The Minister or elder should address the following questions to the candidate(s) whose reply may be by verbal assent or by raising the hand." Following this is a thirteen-point vow which includes these points: "(6) Do you accept the Ten Commandments as the transcript of the character of God and a revelation of His will? Is it your purpose by the power of the indwelling Christ to keep this law, including the fourth commandment, which requires the observance of the seventh day of the week as the Sabbath of the Lord and the memorial of Creation? (8) Do you accept the biblical teaching of spiritual gifts and believe that the gift of prophecy is one of the identifying marks of the remnant church? (11) Do you know and understand the fundamental Bible principles as taught by the Seventh-day Adventist Church? Do you purpose, by the grace of God to fulfill His will by ordering your life in harmony with these

massive plagiarism of Ellen White or the suppression of her early writings.

Not only are Adventists somewhat misleading in their evangelistic approach, their history is literally riddled with deceptive practices which continue to this day. When honest Adventist leaders learned of some of these errors and left the church, they were usually castigated and given over to Satan.[4] In fact, Ellen White went so far as to state,

> When the power of God testifies [has told Ellen White] as to what is truth, that truth is to stand forever as the truth. No after suppositions contrary to the light God has given are to be entertained.[5]

In other words, once Ellen White has clearly supported a given Adventist teaching, based upon a "vision" or "instruction" from "God", that teaching is to stand forever. One now understands how difficult it will be for Adventists to admit error, especially the foundational, fundamental doctrines upon which this church was founded and which received the prophetic stamp of Ellen White's approval.

Adventists know the problems associated with their doctrines, especially their investigative judgment doctrine. When working on their Bible commentary, Adventist scholars became acutely aware that this doctrine had no biblical basis. In fact, a super-secret committee of Adventism's top scholars was appointed by General Conference President, R. R. Figuhr, to solve their Daniel 8:14/1844 problem. This committee of Adventist scholars worked on

---

principles? (13) Do you accept and believe that the Seventh-day Adventist Church is the remnant church of Bible prophecy and that people of every nation, race and language are invited and accepted into its fellowship? Do you desire to be a member of this local congregation of the world church?"

[4] *Spiritual Gifts,* Vol. 1, p. 135, 136, 139, 140, 144, 152, 152; *Cultic Doctrine,* p. 187, 188.

[5] Ellen G. White, *Loma Linda Manuscript* No. 150.

this problem for five years, could not solve it, disbanded, left no minutes and were instructed to continue to teach the investigative judgment based upon their "traditional assumptions."[6,7] The church has tried to make it appear this problem has been solved by publishing a huge, multivolume "scholarly work." However, it is riddled with assumptions. The late Dr. Raymond Cottrell was Adventism's best Hebrew scholar; he sat on the secret committee and wrote the SDA commentary on Daniel. He concluded that this series was little more than "obscurantism", designed to make things appear different from what they really are[8]—a good definition of deception.

According to one member of SDAs Biblical Research Committee, it either tended to ignore serious questions about Adventist doctrine, or it would turn the problem over to a naïve scholar who would defend without question the traditional teaching.

> If someone presented a paper pointing toward a conclusion at variance with the church's teaching it was just as quickly relegated to the denomination's archival collection, never to surface again.[9]

Cultic Doctrine lists and illustrates seventeen ways Adventists have dealt with known error. Yet the church has never, to this author's knowledge, publicly admitted doctrinal error. The reason being it would create a crisis of faith among its members who believe the historic teachings of Adventism.[10]

---

[6] *Cultic Doctrine*, Chapter, "Lumps Under the Rug."

[7] Remember there are 22 assumptions needed to support this doctrine as taught by Ellen White. Most of these are contrary to the evidence.

[8] http://www.ratzlaf.com/pdf%20files/Cottrell%201844.pdf

[9] In personal conversations with Jerry Gladson, Ph. D. a former member of the committee.

[10] See *Cultic Doctrine,* Chapter 11, for a complete list and explanation.

Before I reprinted *Cultic Doctrine* I wrote a certified letter to the general conference president asking him if Adventists still supported some of the early erroneous Adventist teachings. True to the template motioned before, he never responded.

Dr. Gerhard Pfandl wrote the Sabbath School lessons for the fourth quarter of 2004, which were a study of the book of Daniel. He followed the traditional Adventist interpretation. Eduardo Martínez-Rancaño, another Adventist scholar, recognized the numerous assumptions, blatant errors and misuse of Scripture in these lessons. Eduardo wrote a detailed letter to Dr. Pfandl in November, 2004, asking questions, giving insight to the biblical text and pointing out his misuse of Scripture. The letter was not answered, so on March 12, 2005, Eduardo spoke personally to General Conference President, Jan Paulsen, about this letter. Elder Paulsen expressed his surprise that Dr. Pfandl hadn't answered. Following the same template, no answer was ever forthcoming. Since these leaders are most unwilling to face this issue, this letter with the author's permission, is now posted on the internet so that the public will be aware of the indefensible position the SDA church holds on their interpretation of Daniel and their "sanctuary" doctrine.[11]

Some Adventists claim that the church has changed and it no longer believes its old historical errors. However, all such talk is untrue. President Jan Paulson, stated:

Take specifically our understanding of judgment and Christ's ministry in the heavenly sanctuary and the prophetic messages in which these teachings are contained. Some are suggesting that since the 1980 (Glacier View) meetings, the very teachings that the church affirmed that year at those meetings have been abandoned, and that the church has essentially moved to

---

[11] www.LifeAssuranceMinistries.com Click on "Articles".

accept the very positions it rejected then. Such a claim is a distortion of reality, and nothing could be further from the truth. The historic sanctuary message, based on Scripture and supported by the writings of Ellen White, continues to be held to unequivocally. And the inspired authorities on which these and other doctrines are based, namely the Bible supported by the writings of Ellen White, continue to be the hermeneutical foundation on which we as a church place all matters of faith and conduct. Let no one think that there has been a change of position in regard to this.[12]

A careful reading of the above statement confirms that the SDA church has not changed its historic doctrines. Neither does if offer much hope for future change. Note that these doctrines are based on "the inspired authorities" (plural)—the Bible as interpreted by Ellen White. It may be true that some Adventists no longer believe SDA's historical doctrines; nevertheless these doctrines remain the official teachings of the church.

Most Adventists who tell evangelicals they no longer believe in the investigative judgment, or other errors of Adventism, will not publically renounce these errors.

---

[12] http://www.adventistreview.org/2002-1524/story3.html

Chapter
ELEVEN

Author's Summary Remarks

At this writing the author is heavily involved in ministry to questioning, transiting and former Seventh-day Adventists and is now also working with evangelical pastors. A few personal, closing remarks are in order.

When I left the Adventist church in 1981 I felt I should never write anything against the SDA church. After doing a thorough, inductive study of the Sabbath, I reached the conclusion that Sabbath observance was not required or even expected of new covenant believers. I noticed that many Adventists were leaving the SDA church but few were finding Christian fellowship in other churches. Many became agnostic and threw out the proverbial "baby with the bathwater". I wrote *Sabbath in Crisis,* now enlarged and re-titled *Sabbath in Christ* to help former Adventists make the difficult transition into churches which worship on Sunday.

Some years later, I was introduced to *The Clear Word Bible,* now titled *The Clear Word.* When I read Daniel 8:14 in this "Bible" I could not believe that the church I grew up in and pastored in would ever resort to such deceptive corruption. Something swelled up inside of me that said, "This must stop!" I did not leave my position as pastor in the Adventist church until I had done a through, in-depth study of Adventist's sanctuary theology. I *knew* it was an unbiblical doctrine that undermined the gospel. And I also *knew* that Adventist leaders were well aware of this fact and had covered it up time and again. Now, with the publication of *The Clear Word Bible,* Adventists would be led to believe their sanctuary theology was biblical.

That experience motivated me to write *Cultic Doctrine.* When I wrote that book I was not yet prepared to call the Adventist church a cult even though it met the majority of the criteria. I continued to pray that the SDA church would openly face the errors of its doctrinal teachings and fully accept the truths of Scripture and embrace the simple new convent gospel. From all indications, however, the leadership of the church has become more firmly entrenched into its cultic past than it was some years ago.

My dear SDA mother passed away in 2006 at the age of 99. In her belongings I found *The Clear Word* in which she had underlined passages in red pencil from Genesis to Revelation. Yes, Daniel 8:14 was included. She died in the deception of believing SDA's sanctuary theology[1] was biblical. She, like millions of other SDAs, trusted Adventist scholars to be honest.

I have seen the way that Adventist leaders have dealt with the hundreds of Adventist pastors and the thousands of members who have refused to believe or teach the unbiblical doctrines of the SDA church. I have personally spoken with many of them. Most of these have been expelled from the ministry and/or disfellowshipped and labeled as "apostates" even though they continue to be strong believers in Christ and in the teachings of the Bible.

Many Adventist members seem to have the same cultic mentality. I have personally received letters addressed "to the church of Satan" sent to my home. I have also received hundreds, if not thousands, of obscene letters and emails

---

[1] As well as the other unbiblical doctrines of the SDA church.

condemning me to burn in hell and telling me that there is no hope for my salvation unless I repent and return to the "true, remnant Seventh-day Adventist church."[2]

Based upon these practices, the continued promotion of *The Clear Word* and the errors of Adventism as officially taught and practiced as outlined in this book, it is with deep regret and sorrow that I now feel compelled to include the Adventist church in the kingdom of the cults.

I recognize that the term "cult" does not fit every Seventh-day Adventist. However, the fact that the Seventh-day Adventist church *officially* continues to refuse to renounce past errors and continues to hold to a mixture of truth and error puts it, I feel, outside the realm of evangelical Christianity. Mixing truth with error—error which compromises the gospel—only makes the embedded error more dangerous because it is less apparent.

After again watching the interview with the late Walter Martin and William Johnson on the John Ankerberg show I am convinced that if Walter Martin were alive today he would do the same. I believe Dr. Martin had already made the change in his mind but died before he could make the change in print. I encourage the reader to watch this insightful series of interviews. Find them on the internet at: http://www.ankerberg.com or LAM Publications website at: http://www.lifeassuranceministries.com/svideolam.html

---

[2] Find a small sampling of these letters in *Proclamation!* under Letters to the Editor. Also read the Mail Boxes on my internet website at http://www.lifeassuranceministries.com/mailbox.html

Truly, truly,
I say
to you,
he who
believes
has
eternal life

Chapter
TWELVE

The Good News of Christ

The mission of Life Assurance Miniseries is to proclaim the good news of the new covenant gospel of grace in Christ and to combat the errors of legalism and false religion.

We believe that all have sinned in the past and we all continue to fall short of God's ideal (Rom. 3:23). God is not willing that any perish but wishes all to come to repentance (2 Pet. 3). He loved the world so much that He gave His only begotten Son, that whoever believes in Him should not perish, but have eternal life (Jn. 3:16).

God's offer of salvation is for "whoever believes". Of ourselves we cannot exercise saving faith, but God in His great mercy gives us both grace and faith to receive His gift (Eph. 2:8, 9; Tit. 3:5). When God reaches down in grace and mercy to us and we in repentance and acknowledgement of our sin receive His free gift of salvation, we are born again, born from above, born of the Spirit in our spirit and become new creatures in Christ Jesus (Jn. 3:3–8; 2 Cor. 5:17).

At this point we are counted perfectly righteous—with the very "righteousness of God" (Rom. 3:21, 22). The "righteousness of God" that is imputed to us who believe is far above the "righteousness of the law" and is not even associated with the "righteousness of the law" (Phil. 3:6; Rom. 4:13; 9:31; 10:4, 5; Gal. 2:21; 3:21; Phil. 3:6–9).

God promised that the "more abundant" Christian life would be a life filled with assurance, peace, rest and joy— and as long as we are in this old world, some persecutions (Jn. 10:10; Heb. 3:14; 6:11; 10:22; 11:1; Jn. 14:27; Mt. 11:28, 29; Jn. 15:11; Mk. 10:30).

It makes a monumental difference on where the Christian life is focused. Living with a "law focus" has only two consequences: either one is always under guilt and condemnation for falling short of God's ideal; or one deceives himself into thinking that he has fully obeyed. Usually when the latter happens the law focused person will set up arbitrary rules that define accepted obedience.[1] Then when he feels he has kept the rules well enough he becomes judgmental of others who do not measure up to his understanding of what is required. However, there is a better way!

Look Away!

By contrast, however, the new covenant gospel provides a better way.[2] We are not under law; we are dead to the law, and the law no longer plays any function in our salvation. "For Christ is the end of the law for righteous-

---

[1] This is the hallmark of legalism. Take Sabbath keeping for example. Many Sabbatarians believe they are keeping the Sabbath because they measure up to the Sabbath rules that are accepted in their group, church or denomination. If Seventh-day Adventists claim to believe what they say they believe, then they are under obligation to keep *all* the biblical Sabbath laws, plus those laid down By Ellen White. See *Sabbath in Christ,* pages 74–76 for a list of the biblical rules for Sabbath keeping and pages 388–392 for a partial list of Sabbath rules laid down by Ellen White.

[2] The writer of Hebrews shows over and over again how the new covenant is "better" than the old. See Heb. 1:4; 6:9; 7:19, 22; 8:6; 9:23; 10:34; 11:4, 16, 35, 40; 12:24.

ness to everyone who believes."[3] Rather than look back to the law for sanctified living, as the Galatians did, Christians are to look away from the law and focus their attention on what God has already done for them, what He promises to continue to do for them and what He now declares about them.

The following verses contain so much good news, especially for those of us who have gown up on law; one sometimes has to read a verse several times to comprehend its scope and truthfulness. I encourage you to underline these verses in your Bible.[4] Memorize them and they will become your "sword of the Spirit" to vanquish all the fiery temptations of the devil. When you read them in the following paragraph, do not rush from one statement to the next; rather let the truth of each Scripture sink into your soul and spirit. Here is the power of the gospel. Here is the power of the Spirit-filled life. Here is where one finds hilarious joy that is constant in the face of difficulties. Here is the good news that is not only to be received but must be proclaimed. Here is our foundation of faith. Here is the engine that drives Life Assurance Ministries.

The writer of Hebrews says, "There remains therefore a Sabbath rest for the people of God." He admonishes us to "be diligent to enter that rest." And he says "we who have believed enter that rest"[5] (Heb. 4:3, 9, 11). Christians who believe enter the "rest" of fellowship with God, the "rest" of Eden's seventh day when all was very good. We now have eternal life (Jn. 6:47). We now *know* we have eternal

---

[3] Rom. 10:4.

[4] I have left the references in the text to make it easier to review these in your Bible.

[5] In Greek, "believed" is written in such a way that it refers to something that takes place in an instant of time. For a thorough study of this passage, see *Sabbath in Christ,* "The Rest that Remains".

life (1 Jn. 5:13). We now have peace with God (Rom. 5:1). We now have been reconciled to God (Rom. 5:10). Our old self (man) was crucified with Christ (Rom. 6:6). We are now to consider ourselves to be dead to sin (Rom. 6:11). We are now freed from sin (Rom. 6:18, 22; 1 Jn. 3:8, 9). We are now dead to the law (Rom. 7:4). We now have been released from the law (Rom. 7:6). We now serve in the newness of the Spirit and not in the oldness of the letter (Rom. 7:6). There is now no condemnation to those who are in Christ Jesus (Rom. 8:1). We have now received the spirit of adoption (Rom. 8:15). We now overwhelmingly conquer through Him who loved us (Rom. 8:37). We are now sealed with the Holy Spirit of promise (Eph. 1:13). We are now saved through faith (Eph. 2:8). We are now the dwelling of the Holy Spirit (Eph. 2:22). We are now chosen in Christ (Eph. 1:4). We now have redemption through his blood (Eph. 1:7). God is now at work in us to will and to do His good pleasure (Phil. 2:13). We are now qualified to share in the inheritance of the saints in light (Col. 1:12). We have now been transferred to the kingdom of His beloved Son (Col. 1:13).We now have each received a spiritual gift (Rom. 12; 1 Cor. 12; Eph. 4). The Spirit now helps our weaknesses (Rom. 8:26). We have now been predestined to be like Christ (Rom. 8:29). I invite you to read these Scriptures day after day until you internalize what God's Word declares about your standing in Christ.

Reframe your faith

Too often we speak flippantly about "believing" as if it were something of little consequence. We rightly interpret faith as "trusting Christ alone for salvation." However, my goal in concluding this book is to encourage you to expand and reframe your concept of faith not only to include "trusting Christ alone for salvation" but also to include

ALL the many promises of God and the things that God now declarers to be true about the believing Christian. If we truly believe every biblical statement in the foregoing paragraph, we will find a new identity. We will discover that we really are new creatures in Christ Jesus. We will find that we now have the very righteousness of God which comes by faith in Christ Jesus because God has declared it so. We turn from the slavery of "do" to the freedom of "done"; from the striving to become to the assurance of God's declaration.

> But their minds were hardened; for until this very day at the reading of the old covenant the same veil remains unlifted, because it is removed in Christ. But to this day whenever Moses is read, a veil lies over their heart; but whenever a person turns to the Lord, the veil is taken away. Now the Lord is the Spirit, and where the Spirit of the Lord is, there is liberty. But we all, with unveiled face, beholding as in a mirror the glory of the Lord, are being transformed into the same image from glory to glory, just as from the Lord, the Spirit (2 Cor. 3:14–18).

Be diligent to present yourself approved to God as a workman who does not need to be ashamed, handling accurately the word of truth

Suggested Resources

LAM Publications, LLC

P.O. Box 11587, Glendale, AZ 85318 | Phone: 800-355-7073 | Email: dale@ratzlaf.com

If possible, order online. We accept most major credit cards on our secure server. Go to: www.LifeAssuranceMinistries.com Then click on "Bookstore".

Listed below are books published and/or sold by LAM Publications, LLC. As this is a dynamic list, we suggest that you visit our website listed above for current inventories, prices, package sales and more in-depth descriptions. Prices and availability are subject to change without notice.

Sabbath in Christ—by Dale Ratzlaff, 442 pages, $14.95, ISBN 0-9627546-1-7. This is an easy to read, thorough, biblical study of the gospel, the old and new covenants, and the Sabbath. *Sabbath in Christ* is endorsed by John MacArthur and many other theologians and pastors. "Dale Ratzlaff has done us a real service in providing the best all-around treatment of the Sabbath question to date." Jerry Gladson, Ph.D.

The Cultic Doctrine of Seventh-day Adventists: An Evangelical Resource, An Appeal to SDA Leadership—by Dale Ratzlaff, 388 pages, $14.95, ISBN 0-9627546-9-2. This book reviews the early beginnings of the Seventh-day Adventist Church. It documents how Ellen White—the prophetess of the SDA church—gave a glowing, comprehensive endorsement of William Miller's Bible study methods, his conclusions, and his message, and then lists Miller's fifteen "biblical proofs" that Christ would return in 1843. It follows the flip-flop teachings of the "shut door" of mercy, listing facts unknown to many SDAs and evangelicals. It traces the development of the SDA doctrine of the cleansing of the heavenly sanctuary and the investigative judgment—Adventism's unique "contribution" (they say) to Christianity. It then contrasts this SDA doctrine with the biblical teaching of the judgment and the gospel.

Truth Led Me Out—by Dale Ratzlaff, 152 pages, $10.00. ISBN 0-9747679-5-6. This is a gripping narrative life story of Ratzlaff's journey from being a fourth generation Seventh-day Adventist to simply being "a Christian". For the sake of history, Ratzlaff includes names, places, events and the information that caused him to leave Adventism. The reader is pulled into the story and must face the difficult decision: teach error with a promising future, or be cast out. For the sake of history a number of cartoons describing the ongoing crisis in Adventism are included.

A Theologian's Journey from Seventh-day Adventism to Mainstream Christianity—by Jerry Gladson, Ph.D., 388 pages, $14.95, ISBN 0-9627546-4-1. Dr. Gladson was an SDA theologian, professor and pastor serving an important role at the central core of Adventist scholarship for many years. Drawing from his meticulously kept journals, Dr. Gladson describes events at the center of the crisis in Adventism.

White Out—by Dirk Anderson, 160 pages, $9.95, ISBN 0-9627546-5X. This is another must-read book for those who want to know the full truth about Ellen White. Mr. Anderson has compiled many historical documents about Ellen White and early Adventism. He compares these records with those passed down by the SDA denomination.

Discovering the New Covenant—Why I am no Longer a Seventh-day Adventist—by Greg Taylor, 160 Pages, $10.00, ISBN 0-9747670-0-5. Greg Taylor shares how his life was changed when, through careful Bible study, he discovered the truth of the new covenant. Then he saw that Adventist theology did not line up with the new covenant truth.

White Washed—Uncovering the Myths of Ellen G. White—by Sydney Cleveland, 230 pages, $12.95, ISBN 0-9627546-8-4. Pastor Cleveland shows beyond a shadow of a doubt that the writings of Ellen White disagree with Scripture on a number of points, including some fundamental to faith.

Life of Mrs. E.G. White, Seventh-day Adventist Prophet, Her False Claims Refuted—by D. M. Canright, 291 pages, $12.95, ISBN 0-9664531-0-7. This was written the year of Canright's death in 1919. It fills in many missing gaps in SDA history—gaps which the Adventist church would like to forget.

The Sabbath and the Lord's Day—by H. M. Riggle, 160 pages, $7.95. This is an old book but remains an easy to read, excellent resource for those who want more biblical answers to the Sabbath question.

Daniel 8:14, The Day of Atonement and The Investigative Judgment—by Desmond Ford, Ph. D., 600 pages, $15.00. This book contains material not easy to come by elsewhere. While some parts are difficult to read, those who want to do a thorough study of this topic will find this invaluable source material.

The White Lie—by Walter T. Rea, Ph.D., 409 pages $15.00. This is a well-documented work proving beyond the shadow of doubt that much, if not most, of the writings of Ellen White were copied from others. That which she claims to have received from God in vision often can be traced to the works of others. Dr. Rea has shown that from 50-90 percent of the writings of Ellen White were plagiarized from others.

E-Books

Bible Answers to Sabbath Questions—Verle Streifling, Ph. D., 470 pages $10.00. This is a pre-publication version of Dr. Streifling's comprehensive new book on the topic of the Sabbath. It will be emailed to those who purchase it. This work on the Sabbath lets the Bible define its terms as "creative days", God's resting, the one law, etc. It examines the alleged support for Sabbath keeping in the New Testament, using valid hermeneutics, with unique insights on Hebrews 3 and 4.

As In A Mirror—Fred Mazzaferri, Ph. D., 320 pages $10.00. This is a scholarly study of SDA's sanctuary/judgment theology for those who use Greek and Hebrew. This is not bedtime reading. Regardless, this careful critique by a well informed scholar is an extremely valuable resource for the serious Bible student seeking to comprehend Seventh-day Adventism.

Cleansing God's Sanctuaries—Fred Mazzaferri, Ph. D, 103 pages, $10.00. A study of SDA's sanctuary/judgment theology for those who do not have a working knowledge of the original languages. Here is a book that has long been needed.

A Biblical Study of the Lord's Day—Rodney Nelson, 131 pages, $5.00. Rodney shows that while Sunday, the Lord's Day is not another "Sabbath", it nevertheless is an important day for Christians.

Español: Libros acerca de temas bíblicos.

Sábado en Cristo, de Dale Ratzlaff, $15.00 (USA) ISBN 0-9747679-2-1, traducido por Ben Escalante.

La doctrina sectaria de los adventistas del séptimo día, $15.00 (USA). ISBN 0-9747679-3-X, Este libro es solo para los que desean conocer la verdad y no temen descubrir verdades que los harán libres. Rey G. Cantú y William E. Castillo.

La nube blanca, de Dirk Anderson, $9.95 (USA), ISBN 0-747679-1-3.

La verdad acerca de la "verdad" de los adventistas del séptimo día, de Dale Ratzlaff, $3.95 ISBN 0-9627546-3-3.

Websites on Adventism

www.LifeAssuranceMinistries.com Books, CDs and articles by former SDAs including former SDA pastors and theologians.

www.LifeAssuranceMinistries.org is the website for Life Assurance Ministries, Inc., publisher of *Proclamation!*

www.FormerAdventist.com is the site for the Former Adventist Forum and annual former Adventist conferences.

www.EllenWhiteExposed.com, or www.EllenWhite.org This site has extensive material on Ellen G. White's errors.

www.ExAdventist.com This is the site of a large ministry to inquiring and transitioning Adventists.

www.TruthOrFables.com Hundreds of pages of valuable information on the errors of Adventism and current events dealing with Adventism.

www.ThinkAboutEternity.org This site is dedicated to ministry to the cults, including Mormonism, Adventism, and Jehovah Witnesses.

www.OneFlockMinistries.org This site is run by Pastor Greg Taylor who fosters a ministry in Africa to help former Adventist pastors as they transition from Adventism into evangelical churches.

www.Watchman.org Watchman Fellowship is well known for its apologetic ministry to the cults.

www.MacGregorMinistries.org This site is probably the best site for working with Jehovah Witnesses. They also have a large section dealing with Adventism and other cults.

www.adventist.org The official website for the Seventh-day Adventist Church.